Spells

Spells

21st-Century Occult Poetry

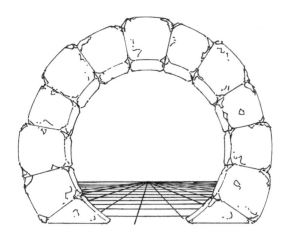

edited by
Sarah Shin and Rebecca Tamás

'Prayer' by Kaveh Akbar, published in *Calling a Wolf a Wolf* (Alice James, 2017), is reproduced by permission of the author.

'Augury' by Nuar Alsadir, published in *More Shadow than Bird* (Salt, 2012), is reproduced by permission of the author and publisher.

'Canopy' by Emily Berry, published in *Stranger, Baby* (Faber & Faber, 2017), is reproduced by permission of the author and publisher.

'Camisado' by CAConrad, published in *The Scores*, is reproduced by permission of the author.

From 'The Hermit' by Lucy Ives, published in *The Hermit* (Song Cave, 2016), is reproduced by permission of the author.

'My Narrative Costume is a Witch Without Reputation' by Amy Key, published in *Isn't Forever* (Bloodaxe Books, 2018), is reproduced by permission of the author and publisher.

'Come to Dust' from *So Far So Good* is reproduced by kind permission of the Estate of Ursula K Le Guin.

'If I Were A Buddhist I'd Chant for Your Happiness' by Karen McCarthy Woolf, published in *NW15: The Anthology of New Writing* edited by Bernardine Evaristo and Maggie Gee (Granta, 2007), is reproduced by permission of the author.

A version of 'Thursday' by Ariana Reines was published in *Spork* (2012) and is reproduced by permission of the author.

First published by Ignota 2018
This selection © Ignota 2018
The contributions © the contributors 2018

1 3 5 7 9 10 8 6 4 2

Ignota
ignota.org

ISBN-13: 978-1-9996759-0-5

Design by Cecilia Serafini
Illustration by Soraya Gilanni
Typeset in Electra by Lindsay Nash
Printed and bound in Great Britain by TJ International

Contents

The Broken Open

Magic exists in most societies in one way or another, and one of the forms it exists in a lot of places is, if you know a thing's true name, you have power over the thing, or the person. And of course it's irresistible because I'm a writer. I use words, and knowing the names of things is – I do magic, I do make up things that didn't exist before by naming them.

Ursula K. Le Guin, *Worlds of Ursula K. Le Guin*
(dir. Arwen Curry, 2018)

In the beginning was the Word.

No.

This is about the moment before the word, when everything inside you is broken open.

Words, together; multiple and multivalent, coming in a rush, sounding in a chorus, a force like a waterfall. A dam breaking. A difficult birth.

*

The word 'witch' enters written English in c.890, according to the Oxford English Dictionary, to mean a man practising sorcery ('wicca', weak masculine). It is another hundred years before it is used – in writing – with its more familiar gendered dimension: witch from 'wicce' (feminine). Where does it come from? Old English *wiccian*, from the German *wicken*, *wikken*. 'Of obscure origin.'

Obscure origins are, often, in an undocumentable language spoken, down the generations, far from the privilege of writing. In *wikken* we can perhaps hear a whisper of the German word *wissen*, knowledge; *wikken* might indicate an alternate form of knowing, one given into earth and heard in the sky.

Khairani Barokka writes backwards and forwards from this difficult birth, of the knowledge birthed in its difficulty, in her spell-poem:

> Chani knows the term is archaic, gives its history
> for mystifying chart, points to femmeness and creative wombs
> broken, bust open, diminished. Disrespected, pushed,
>   slapped red to know one's place by muscly hands.

To know one's place becomes a profound art, in the broken open. It takes this density of words, their history.
This isn't about God making the world with the Word. It's about the witches who've been remaking the world, unmaking the mess he made, ever since that difficult birth.

*

To be a witch, then, is to know words. To be a witch is to know, in your bones (your tired bones), where the word 'witch' might come from. Birth stories, origin myths, are wandering and plural, partial but yours. Not someone else's definition of your self, but what you have learned through dangers untold and hardships unnumbered. The thing you have to tell, have to say.

Listen to Canisia Lubrin sing of the origins and the journey in 'Geology Lesson 4':

she just them bones she was
born with, is all, took with her
a dominion of horns and spell
books, and seven recited rants

How to take everything it takes (with you when you leave). How to
work the 'and' between books and rants, the written and the sung.
How to spell it, over and over again, until it is heard.

❊

It's irresistible, as the great mage Ursula K. Le Guin, who appears
herein in the guise of one of her last poems, says. To conjure with
words, with the right words, as editors Sarah Shin and Rebecca
Tamás write:

> Spells are poems; poetry is spelling. Spell-poems are vehicles
> of change that take us beyond the borders of the rational into
> a place where the right words can influence the universe.

Summoning hexes and feminism for *Spells*, they called (for writers
and voices from) the four corners and six directions, in recogni-
tion of a 'pluralistic magical language' that provides 'sacred spaces
away from everyday experience of violence and harassment.' Not
an escape, but 'a space for healing and liberation', working on the
physical body, the affective body, the thinking body, and the subtle
body of the spirit. Spells to call these four bodies together, against
a world that pushes them apart and fractures them. Spells for what
has been broken, open.

❊   ❊   ❊

And then we are in the open. It is an enchanted space.

Let us revive, in the English language, the tradition of being enchanted when we meet each other. *Enchanté/e, encantadx*, that charmed greeting in French or Spanish. Let us delink it from the tired old rituals of courtship and make it anew, the sign of witch meeting witch.

Let us mean it. Let us mean the enchantment of taking care, which is where writing and magic meet: care that begins in the right words for things, in the chant that sings in *enchanted*. What poetry can do if we let it – take care of us.

Enchanted to be here. Only such spells as Shin and Tamás are capable of working could bring us together – and make no mistake, it is work to summon and enfold such jostling, dancing, protesting, loving spirits. Across the time and space of silencing, of fear, of separation, of loss, we have come together. Make no mistake: when we encounter such voices – feminist, queer, decolonial, dis/abled – there is magic at play beyond even the ordinary, practical magic of writing and publishing, the dilation of time and instant connections between writer and reader.

Be gentle, take care with these words as the writers have taken care with them. Take the care they offer you in their chant, their rhythms and movement, their caress of the surface of language. To stand with us in this circle with its centre everywhere and its circumference now/here is to be under a spell. A pleasure to meet you here: enchanted.

Enchantment is vulnerable. Vulnerability is enchantment. Enchantment, like vulnerability, is necessary.

We are living in the broken open. So much has piled on to us that we push back. The crush is so intense that we cry out.

We are open: we are broken.

*

Hoa Nguyen opens her spell-poem with an immediate invocation of the real violence that has broken us open. If we accept the power of words, then we feel the stabs in our bodies:

Mouth wet with life
& stabbed
    Stabbed and staggered
        three times of knives

as three literal people

    stab me metaphorically
        in Greenbelt Maryland

Trauma remains in the body – the mind-body. It could be said that trauma, painfully, reveals that body is also mind, affect, spirit; that all four meet at the point of the knives. This is not to endorse the violence, but to mark how far we have come from living in our multiple, attuned bodies.

Trauma is, in or behind many of these spells, the broken open: the realisation of how great is the need to find the right words to record and to transform; how great is the power inside us, the power that the violence comes to steal and erase.

*

That anything of what could broadly be called witchcraft survives – other than what was said of it by inquisitors and torturers – is evidence that it works; that it continues to conjure and enchant, even when suppressed. We could say it survived by hiding, but that's only partially true. It survived in the broken open, in the wounds of trauma, as memory does. It survived by arising at need, and by being difficult: localised, specific, demanding, resistant, persistent. In repetitions and in the echoes of rituals.

In '1947: Spell to Reverse a Line', Bhanu Kapil calls us with a simple ritual, to make a place to meet; the place where the sum total of the world that makes the poet was broken open, the place of Partition and great pain:

> If the line is a border and a border is a boundary award.
>
> If you left at night.
>
> If you were warned by your neighbours.
>
> If you saw through a hole in the cart…
>
> And if this glimpse repeated on loop, a story of early childhood woven into bed-time fairy-tales and stories.
>
> Then this is a spell to reverse the line, the hole, the night itself.

Witchcraft – like the violence it opposes – works by repetition, by the looping and looping and looping of a thread, by the network of words. Kapil's line is a reminder that textiles and text are connected. Textiles, historically the preserve of women, predate architecture. The loom was the first computer. Plaids may encode calendars. The first clay figurines found in Turkey and the Balkans wear fringed kilts whose knots, like the Quechua *quipu* or *khipu*, may be records, journals, messages – or spells.

Recording history is, after all, itself a spell. Knotting, stitching, and weaving are enduring metaphors for how poems, in particular, work themselves. Kapil shows us the underside of the cloth, the work, where the process and the programme become one and we see the trace of the body doing (or undoing) itself. Radical self-love.

*

Moving only at their own pace, spell-poems do not just record history, but reorder it, reorganise it into new lines that reveal the obscured. They change time, reminding us of the phrase 'for a spell.' Poems slow us down, dance us to their rhythm, turn time from a line to a circle.

Or a prism; refracting their thoughts through elemental crystals. Francesca Lisette sees, through rose quartz, the facet of time that ritual seeks; its specificity and singularity vibrating outwards ad infinitum:

> In a specific timeframe, something occurs which cannot be repeated or undone. Each reading is a ritual. It is also a performance. It is also a gift.
>
> Because the body is more than a frame. It is a vibration.

Where does a spell begin and end? What do its effects look like if we move in the time of poetry, that long cycle that stretches back into 'obscure origins' and forward into transformative resurgence? What if we come to our elemental selves of earth, air, fire, and water (in the European tradition), to the vibrations that make volcanoes and waves, gentle breezes and earthquakes.

If a spell is a crystal, it holds compacted, geological time. Lisette's spell-poem asks: How can such vast histories be made to reverberate? How can the traumatic memories of their formation be released, with a healing scintillance?

*

Words, like crystals – like water – hold a density of memory that detonates inside us. Erica Scourti's spell-poem 'Lost to the Phosphorus' tests spit and Smart Water to see if these liquids can hold the two languages, two alphabets, of her fluid-filled body, 'sweat and salt', English and Greek, together. 'What are your symptoms?' she is asked, and so asks us. Scourti re-sounds the Mediterranean origins of English words, a reminder that here is linked to there. We are inextricable. Words bind us, together.

And where do we go from there? Scourti concludes:

> I'm no good at endings- too prone to clichés-
> because kaimos, then metaphrasetai-
> but I wanted you to come away with something
> to hold
> a protective shell,
> glowing in a sweaty palm
> a skinful reminder

The shell is in your hand, she says. Listen. Sing.

*

Magic comes down the line: feel the sweet frisson, the freight of responsibility. The right words are imbued with power by the righteousness of those who spoke them before us. We sing humbly to continue their great songs.

Through the lines of this spell-book, we raise a chorus for Audre Lorde, lifelong activist, writer, and speaker of secret truths to power, who wrote of a singular bus journey in her memoir *Zami: A New Spelling of My Name*:

the angelic orchestration swelled, filling my head with the sharpness and precision of the words; the music was like a surge of strength. It felt rich with hope and a promise of life – more importantly, a new way through or beyond pain.

I'll die this death on Calvary
ain't
gonna
die
no
more!

The physical realities of the dingy bus slid away from me. I suddenly stood upon a hill in the center of an unknown country, hearing the sky fill with a new spelling of my own name.

Lorde offers us a map to that unknown country and a grimoire of its potencies. They are not easy to access – Lorde did not rest. She rode the bus, and wrote poetry there, turning the great wisdom she learned, through struggle, into words we can all read. And by reading, open our ears to that angelic orchestration: that's the magic.

*

Lorde's teaching of radical self-love is founded upon a spell, the original spell: to say your name, magically, and make your true identity.

Karen McCarthy Woolf names one version of herself in 'If I Were a Buddhist I'd Chant for Your Happiness':

I shall propagate Sea Wolfes and watch
them shoot into my own army of glittering
green gargoyles.

Woolf/Wolfe: the flexibility of English, which crackles with homonyms and homophones, with centuries and continents shaping diverse orthographies, a reminder that what is written is an echo of what is spoken or sung – a 'glittering' shape on a page that binds the voice into a spell.

*

It is time to return the words to those whose mouths know their shapes. Those who sing them so we can listen, and perhaps be changed. In 'For Those Who Mispronounce My Name', Kayo Chingonyi offers a spell as an act of profound kindness borne of self-love. A healing spell against the violence of misnaming, against the accounting of origins as 'obscure'. The spell extends out to the reader/listener who does not speak the Bantu language of Luvale, because it first intends inwards, finding the person

who does not exist according
to your version of events.

*

Did no one tell you
naming is a magical act,
words giving shape
to life

In that asterisk between the stanzas is a ritual of transformation: work born from migration and displacement; work of self-location and emplacement, formed on the page to release that voice we now hear, differently.

*

What a spell creates, as you speak it, is you: a sense of your power to create. A spell spells you. Jen Calleja ends her spell-poem with this crucial instruction:

> You just have to mean it
>
> and when I say mean it
>
> I mean: your intention must always be to save your own life.

Read all these words aloud, together, and mean them. Give that gift to the writers who crafted them, and the editors who bound them. Search out more of their work, invoke them in conversation and in your own writing and singing.

Break open the walls, the distance between writer and reader by taking the words into your body, your history. Let them break you open as, together, we enter this unknown country, this decentred centre, this intention to save our lives.

Please, be enchanted. It could save us.

*

I do magic, Le Guin says, simple as elemental.

In their spell-poem, CAConrad says:

> poetry is the opposite of escape
> but makes this world endurable
> how the smallest puddle
> reflects the entire sky

These are the stakes of re-enchantment: the smallest puddle, the entire sky. The relation between each individual being and the ecosystem that we all contain, breathing it, swallowing it. In Conrad's practice of (Soma)tic Rituals, poetry is exactly the opposite of escape because we are doing poetry (or doing magic) the entire time that we have, and live in, a body.

Poetry, or magic, takes charge of intention: of how our name is said, how our bones are held, how we breathe, how we see. It means believing in ourselves: conjuring the belief that our intentions, our actions, matter – not because we are special or gifted, but because here we are, in the world and part of it.

As Conrad continues:

> everything matters because everything
> hurts someone somewhere as it is mattering
> we became all we carried into the mast
> migratory patterns given to the love again

The '-ing' of the present participle weaves a 'migratory pattern': changing time from a past to which we consign wrongs, to a continuous present (in Gertrude Stein's phrase) in which 'it is mattering' and we have to attend.

Repetition matters, as it did when we were children, chanting and singing. Do it again: that's what ritual means. Repeat and repeat until it is in your bones. Read this book in order, then read it by chance, by procedure, by contingence, until it has you by heart, and you can go on.

'Everything / hurts' across the line break, but we keep (s)inging. If we attend, if we intend, it is the repetition, the ongoingness, that breaks us open.

*

Everything
hurts.

And yet.

That is what the magic says. Everything hurts and yet these words clean the wound. Words that will come to you when you are riding the bus, when you are holding a shell, when you are walking a line; when you realise that each of these seemingly ordinary moments can break you open; and in the break, these words arise.

'Rise up in the smoke of the palo santo', Le Guin spells in 'Come to Dust'. Poetry is the opposite of an escape: it gives us a place to be, where we are (doing) magic, because we endure.

> All earth's dust
> has been life, held soul, is holy.

Hold soul, as these words do, when everything / hurts. The memory of earth, in our mouths. In the beginning was, and is, just this.

So Mayer

Prayer

Kaveh Akbar

again I am thinking of self-love   filled with self-love   the stomach
of the girl who ate only hair was filled with hair   they cut
it out when she died   it formed a mold of her stomach   reducing
a life to its most grotesque artifact   my gurgling internal devotion
to myself   a jaw half-formed   there are words
I will not say   the muscle of my face smeared
with clay   I am more than the worry I make   I choose
my words carefully   we now know some angels are more terrifying
than others   our enemies are replaceable   the stones behind their teeth
glow in moonlight   compared to even a small star
the moon is tiny   it is not God but the flower behind God I treasure

Banshee

Rachael Allen

He'll sit in the window
at an innocent date
with wandering hands
over a port-green stool.
There's the kitchen
where I was murdered
where I was delivered
into a weapon with force
like a small model forester
axing up plastic logs
in a red wooden clock
murdered by a man
the sanctity of communion
I was never alone
the heavy smell of blood
misted up past the crockery
and the murdered girls before me
gathered up in plain cotton
the scores of my limbs
and the nub of my treatment
my hair was a clotted
pattern of wallpaper
like a tapestry of rabbits
and we left with my body
but do not forgive

so easily as that.
Tonight I laugh walking
towards his dark house
my head's a dun lantern
with split ends uplifted
my hands are barbed knots
to take it back
for I'm fury with a shell
and I'm petty.
The old boundary walls
where I leaned in the summer
swaying in my peripherals.
I don now a gray sheet
the dusk colour of bonbons
too seem more like a haunting
light pools through the mock-glass
and the door he approaches
the red door approaches

Augury

Nuar Alsadir

The crow knows,
hangs under the sky
with accusatory inflection.

Wit gathers
and is gone to me:
I grow spectral, imitate stone.

Smoke rises
from the mission next door.
A man without a cup paces, starves.

What Chani Nicholas Told Me

Khairani Barokka

The morning my mother gave up
on coaxing me out of her vagina,
after nearly two days, consented
to being cut open, I was born in a placement
speaking to difficulty:
>   *"under the sun's beams".*

I plucked hymns from wading
in the warmth, amniotic sea.
And no one was bearing me out
>   unless my home was sliced in two.

How I see Chani:
Astrologer bursting sun from her bare bones.
Human and emailing to help with a Moon course.
>   I don't crush a lot (just a player).

The stars when I emerged:
Close to the sun.
Venus retrograde, in Aries, twelfth house.
I hear from Chani *Difficulties*. Here: *Fallen woman*.
Chani knows the term is archaic, gives its history
for mystifying chart, points to femmeness and creative wombs
broken, bust open, diminished. Disrespected, pushed,
>   slapped red to know one's place by muscly hands.

I know, Chani, yeah.
Read me like the salvaged medusa of nerves
        my body has become.

She speaks of my birth placement as archetype:
Venus conjunct Sun, retrograde heart of second planet—
"In the myth of Inanna, this is when she dies
in the underworld
        and is reborn."

Sometimes the river with its faint whiff of tombs,
hand in its water, laughing back at abled prisons.
Coming into a thirty-third year of survivorship,
counting from when they slit my belly-sky roof
and placed my heart like an offering—
to burn under Sun's beams, ripping the empyrean,
befitting an epidermal ceiling.
        I'd wanted to stay.

My orbit of all things rebirths itself;
Chani tells me how, but I am ready, and already:
Firmament-heavy. Beaming back at the burning gaseous.
Mouth trying to be kind, fingers grasping
from all my house placements, Taurus rising half-dead,
half-scorned, half-electric, the bull a symbol
of my mother's Minang house, our clan house
back in the Tanah Datar village, its roof shaped as horns.

Canopy

Emily Berry

The weather was inside.

The branches trembled over the glass as if to apologise; then they thumped and they came in.

And the trees shook everything off until they were bare and clean. They held on to the ground with their long feet and leant into the gale and back again.

This was their way with the wind.

They flung us down and flailed above us with their visions and their pale tree light.

I think they were telling us to survive. That's what a leaf feels like anyway. We lay under their great awry display and they tattooed us with light.

They got inside us and made us speak; I said my first word in their language: 'canopy'.

I was crying and it felt like I was feeding. Be my mother, I said to the trees, in the language of trees, which can't be transcribed, and they shook their hair back, and they bent low with their many arms, and they looked into my eyes as only trees can look into the eyes of a person, they touched me with the rain on their fingers till I was all droplets, till I was a mist, and they said they would.

golem

A.K. Blakemore

you tell them not to fuck with you but they'll fuck with you
anyway maybe even fuck you if they can to give you a real reason
to steep your ear in breath they use to fashion some

apology out of a professed attraction to 'difficult' women –

Cleopatra was a cunt for going quietly –
carried out by eunuchs to feel the soft rain on her skin.

go down to the river and make a man with your bare beautiful
hands and knowledge of sacred geometry.

ensoul.
make him a mouth and spit in it.
learn the only boy worth trusting is your rabbi.

The Gift

Jen Calleja

I was born with a gift
passed down from the sirens on my father's side,
the banshee on my mother's:
the protective charm of song.

Once, when only a child,
I made a woman weep from my singing.
My throat closed up not long after that
from a particularly ruthless curse.

Some years ago, at the moment of my certain suffocation,
and not without an amount of effort,
I managed to whisper a lullaby to myself
and it soothed my nerves and body: every knot unravelled,
    I became a river.
I knew then it would always be my greatest source of power

I can increase my potency by sipping on
honey   lemon   hot water
oily black coffee
gaseous black tea
cortado, water of the coconut
by sucking on
a salt tablet   a birthstone   a lozenge
by snacking on

creamed opals
topped with a trickle of gems: shards of
citrine, aventurine, tourmaline, almandine
negating the produce of the cow, the goat, the sheep.

Even at my most lacklustre I am better than men.
They think it's all about the words –
that mouthing or howling or pronouncing them is enough.

Casting occurs in the space where body and song harmonise.

The catalyst is sincerity, and sincerity requires no specific tone or
volume.

You just have to mean it

and when I say mean it

I mean: your intention must always be to save your own life.

from Blackbox Testing

Vahni Capildeo

If ever I moved to London, it would be for the Thames (not for
you (or you (or you (or a job)))).
Sweet (filthy (historical)) oculus.
Light arrives as the daytime allowance expires. Night arrives, like
the deity dreamers require.
If ~ (Whose angel sucks fire-lozenges (in the silence of candle-
compliant stone (amidst the memorial complaints of sailors
(bruising erasure of cargo)))) If ever ~ (Whose shallows are the
dickens) If ever I moved ~ (Whose dome whispers how roses
glow alongside sunsetting Deptford pinks (multibranch cyclops
showing floribundant (carnation coronations (dogs with eyes the
size of hollow crowns)))) Moved ~ (Whose black depths cradle
(graves (expel (the living)))) For the Thames ~ (I said this would
not take long (but it is (would be) for the Thames)).

Given the chance ~ it skips ~ its spring ~ & enters autumn ~
What skips? ~ It ~ It ~ the best ~ translation can do ~ It ~ the
dream ~ language ~ gestured ~ Skips ~ spring ~ Enters autumn
~ The sea is warm, the earth is warm. The air bites its own tail
~ Ouroboros breeze in an apple tree, the offputting air ~ n'a
rien à dire ~ nothing, you say? ~ Felt want. Night. Ask. I do not
~ speak to thee. ~ Self-want. Night ~ take thy obscureness: ~
task ~ not ~ ask ~ Night runs consonants to vowels ~ starts the
infinite ~ applies day as a finish ~ Stop ~ thy thoughts ~ are ~
donne ~ Summer was dormancy ~ summer as a farmer's town

green dream ~ two peacocks flying ~ away to fly back multiplied
~ The painter painting ~ one peacock over & over ~ aspects
~ iridescence ~ oil ~ mirrors ~ Autumn tanks ~ Autumn's
thankless ~ asks for night ~ dreams ~ with winter ~ I asked night
for a wreath of winter ~ Night ~ feathered a woolf ~ waymarked
a mansfield ~ for how far ~ below sea level ~ vowels ~ classed as
afloat ~ owlcall ~ pleasecomeflying ~ submerged ~

Memory's exiled engineer deposited years of thoughts in
horse-chestnut leaves on Magdalen Bridge that they might
fall into traffic & water & light & wheel back again (just
one more thing (emerald hedgehog egg-bearer) and another
thing (magnolia's rival (candelabra)), like any memory whose
(constancy is inconsistency (constancy is ingathering)) constancy
is outpouring (tu joues? (toujours)), so in this way I dropped
something into the Thames (je ne joue pas), or so I told it
(un jour), so I told it I dropped it (on ne jouera plus), and as I
dropped it (I swear) the Thames told me (it told me so) *je vous le
jure…*

For Those Who Mispronounce My Name

Kayo Chingonyi

After my kakha,
my father's father who died
before I was born,
I was gifted this Luvale name;
the self-same
borne by my kakha, brother
to my father's mother,
who hugged me at Kaunda Airport
because his sister, my kakha,
died before I had a chance to see her again.

*

It is not only my body I've carried
this long while
to the side eye and scrutiny
of border control
but the name your tongue stumbles on
an heirloom
a shibboleth.

*

This is the word for a boy-child
in Darlington whose mother heard my mother

speak this name and wished one day
her son would feel its weight
when she called him
or conjured him in conversation
the way my mother did
— to think I thought myself unloved.

*

What you might think
a simple case of tomato tomato
is life and breath
to somebody like me;
who could search all your histories
and never find his epithet
glowing among those annals and tracts;
who does not exist according
to your version of events.

*

Did no one tell you
naming is a magical act,
words giving shape
to life, life revivified
by utterance,
so long as proper care
is taken to pronounce
the words correctly
thereby completing the spell?

umbra

Elinor Cleghorn

the skin belt holds faster than the bodice.

nightly, the cycle tightens   her whip hand over the whip man

        she was sure the pelt felt smoother in her dreams.

she'll make her journey later; her gallows-tree geography,

claws scored across the lines her mother drew.

*

back then, they called her the living angel; strange spectacle   so full of

light and very feminine;

cynosure of men's coined eyes and grasping hands*

                 (*please refrain from touching the exhibit.)

But her fingers blistered with cunning.

she cricked her joints   *click-click*   *and for my next trick*   micro-flick

her reach   steradian   her resonance   an orbital thrum

forced stimulation   sounds grim in dark weather.

        her belly swelled round something darker still.

crawling like the dogs   she wrested bolt from latch and hastened
heel to heel

no time. the waning sliver could betray her and crack the dawn wide-
open.

too long a subtle body   too flimsy too filmy

lumen he'd called her. *lumen.   mine my light mine my entoptic seraph
my saccade siren my mine remember I made you all by myself out of rods
and cones and I can slam the lid tight shut*

whenever I like –   and babes, there'd be nothing left of you.

*

born *en caul*   born in the waters   never was much of a
swimmer that one, but no matter;

she made a little liquid breather.

for nesting purposes, a blanket bog sufficed   wetland mire for a
bright mare

wait: this is where they harvest the electric

keep still or you'll blow a fuse   and pulverise surprise surprise
the unexpected hits you between the eyes.

nine days her rising time   nursed herself on milkweed   bridled
at her mother's bit.

blasted forth in the middle of the prisoner's cinema double-feature;

mere spent illusion. but lustre is a mineral thing;   Hygeia's dust,
a particular sort of promise.

she grew obscurer, hide-bound, laguno thickened bristles prickles
contra her mother,   that nebulous princess,
        afterimage scorching the slick sheath of the eye-ball.

more moons passed. now she bore a dusky pelage.   it was quite the
wild shroud.
her baby guard-hairs shimmered   but this she kept a secret.
                        and no-body knew she was there

*

night is the shifter's magistrate.   but here we slink above the law.
our ministry governed by the loom-knot the stave the pierced poppet
the *gala* songs   our call to roam

the others simply wear the skin   but mine is all epithelial.
self-cloak cellular   collagen basket-weave

look closer: etched into the hem-lock there's a waveform
sawtooth
mother-tongue transmission
        (an echo only I can hear)

Come the morning I'll clothe it;   feed the children sweep the front
steps
bless the reverend
        but for these few hours our labours must remain invisible

our closeness to the earth is altogether necessary

with soil in our mouths we incant throat music   the glug and growl
makes angels of us all.

They fear our hunger; but we don't need men's blood   we're smooth-
tonged,

inclined toward a different kind of appetite.

the moon is limpid now.

I, born of light and its opposite, will lick my wounds in private.

Camisado

CAConrad

after breaking in
the wolf
calmed
the hens
so he could
take his time with them
twists them open until the right
amount of memory fits into the song
another high price for belonging
poetry is the opposite of escape
but makes this world endurable
how the smallest puddle
reflects the entire sky
a return to every dream
our minds talked us out of
trusting our math of the star
your hand around my shoulder
poet astronaut you know I love you
I have no sense of failure when I am with you
everything matters because everything
hurts someone somewhere as it is mattering
we became all we carried into the mast
migratory patterns given to the love again
a way to end this secrecy of suffering
cut a door in the wolf so we
can retrieve our dead for
a world that matters

Multi/direction Bio/poetics

Nia Davies

What I desired was to join the historic cult of poet-lovers. I would welcome any emperor the tarot foretold. Em*pourer* who comes unelected, who comes as my equal and ruler.

Can I sit you all around me in a circle on a black cloth? Arcane in saliva, your oils are already food for my lungs and can I breath in your discourse? You can all come and touch my solar plexus.

I tried keeping a film of many eyes, many gazes. Kept his smell on the pillow for three days. After the second it went stale. Some licked ears, others anus. Their differing Lacania. I would keep record of a person's constituent auras and vibrations.

But one cannot idealise difference forever before, well, difference. I overboiled with interaction. Laid down. One held my cheeks for years.

You've troubled this conversation into being, I thought, you've taken a beer blonde with my thigh. Can I slit the black cloth we're sitting on and put you in my orbit?

I had strayed into a mania of teeth. Also, a theatre of fluids. Theatre of intersecting narcissisms, poet juice, Bollywood yearning. The saints, my friends, billowing. Their discourse settling in the back of my action.

I tried to answer the questions they asked me truthfully but the voices rang out in their special timbres all container, no content. I tried to let myself contract. Now I lie in a darkened room to become less stimulated.

The word I learnt on this day was 'Scotchie'. So I thought of scotch tape sticky at our borders. Hey, come to the borderlands with me, a friend said.

I corresponded with this ruby counsel who took it to heart. Remembered the word 'metrosexual'. I anointed my bed to change its marital status. The reading rooms glowed with wheat and soil colours.

He asked to be smacked expecting I would choose the right side, but I took the left. I worry that's the wrong hand to take around here. Are you ready? The way to take poetry seriously is you can all come and pull up my cervical spine.

I've noted my flaws, they are hollows in my attention. And when asked, I visualised the multitasking demon, its shaky head and gripping claws. Then, later, the disintegrating owl demon, its grey feather dandruff. There is also the one who cannot give love, it pulls down in a glaucous streak through the organs, hampers the stomach. These all have their constituent allies ready to pull us back in an upwards motion.

But you need to be ready to be pulled up like that. You need to spell some aura of hello helo. Some of these bus journeys are not appropriate for filing invoices, answering emails. Sometimes men read your love letters over your elbows. Others ask you what you are writing because it is so unusual to see a person writing letters on to paper. Or even reading; a man approached me at the carousel to tell me he loved the fact I was reading a book and not a phone like everyone else and I'm staying at the Hotel Trident.

Other men have cared. Other men were 'splaining but I love my father too much to tell them to go. Others yet say they have a scotchie which means they have a woman they have marked as theirs somehow. I still don't understand the meaning of Scotchie.

Which of your demons or allies flushed up to the surface of this spell? Dearest, history surfaces in the blood that colours our lips. I wondered if I should feel all the unfelt shame of the ones who had come from my place before me. Or perhaps it's not possible to carry someone else's unfelt shame. Just the demons wriggling underneath. My love, the worst demon is the one who doesn't love at all. Its colour is slate.

Reflections on shame in sacred spaces

Kate Duckney

My shrine was in the desert.

When my cup and my bowl vanished from the skyline I knew it was
        time to relocate. At sunrise
I throw gasoline over the prayer maze, and then climb into my wagon.
Who would I call at the abbey, besides?

As I ride through the eaten formations, a mirage I am particularly fond
        of looks at me askance
and refuses my blessing. "The cages that you chloroformed are rattling
behind the canvas!" she warns,
and then evaporates.

Perhaps my human credential was my opacity.

At sunset the light is both nasty and nice
in my robe.

Shame shines through me
like the candied sand in a dingo's ear.

*

I decide to build my new shrine in a downstairs bathroom. When I
        arrive in town
there is a pink gall of soap on the mint sink, and a dried sea urchin.

I hold the dried sea urchin in my hand like Claire Foy's orb
whenever I pretend to defecate.

In flux, the nature of equivalent exchange is more and less physical than
     you ever think it will be.
For example the sins of my bad uncle are dessicating inside a loofa; what
     I sacrificed for this
transmutation is hardly chemical.

Absurd New Ways Of Transferring Your Sores To The Silicone

From what I hear at the saloon
there are methods.

*

As it happens, I am lying in a bath of fluorescent oil
listening to a podcast about mothers who keep their children sick.

When you sleep in a bath every night your dreams become indulgent.
     I dreamt that two male pornstars
with tattooed wings were screwing me in midair. Very far below me
     there was a lip-shaped sofa
that I hoped I would land on when they dropped me.

Interpretation is even more indulgent. I think of a painting that is just a
     daschund.

*

In my order nothing is forbidden.
Exile is an electric branch that you take to yourself.

When my shrine stopped being my shrine I did not consider the
        violence that was sent to me, but rather how
I could put distance between myself and the canyon I love, the spiders
cartwheeling down the dune.

I have been evil in my time, but I have also been very good.

In the downstairs bathroom the ornaments are archived and accepted.
        Sometimes I hold a glass tuna
under running water and the life that erupts and thrashes in my hands
        makes me vomit.

At this stage I do not want time to tell.

Bark!

Livia Franchini

> *The business of selling illusions is – wouldn't you say? –*
> *a business that targets vulnerable people.*
>
> *You think so? You really think so, don't you?* [a pause]
> *Then tell me: who, exactly, are these vulnerable people?*
>
> Wanna Marchi, in conversation with Francesca Leosini,
> 'Io sono Vanna Marchi', *Storie Maledette* (Rai3, 2003)

Red mould grew in the tracks of the tiling at the summerhouse out of
   drains
like a clown ghost a bright blood it could follow us around sometimes
a whole afternoon in the heat slide the hem of your vest off one shoulder
or pool salted water in the dent on your lip those days a small distraction
could cost you your fingers permanently stained with the juice of some
   fruit

Illumination seemed to be ubiquitous those days certainly for a few
   years of this
our late childhood in spite of the fact we were growing fast in spite of
moving light from the T.V. to which we composed the number of the
   witch
telemarketing corsets fortunate numbers we were daring each other to
   listen

to the phone ring three times say each other's name three times in the
    mirror

Magic came to us then in short spells from a faraway channel thumbs
    swiped
on a forehead a cross salt stirred into a glass cup unbroken eye contact
    visible sweat
on the edge of a bright flame fingertips dipped in the soft wax of candles
    at dinner
of the red hair of the T.V. presenter her voice the same polish of dark
    ficus leaves
dragged face down on a stone floor the damp outline of a body on the
    pavement

You could always remember all the names of the capitals reluctant to
    drop
the habit of listing them one after the other unprompted the gall of it
she'd been giving us over and over the digits that made up the number
    yet
sitting at the adult table that night you seemed to have forgotten
the numbers counting down from a hundred the exact parameters of it

our available magic

The Hanged Man

Will Harris

He bought a seeded loaf and two ripe and ready avocados
and left them in the hallway, and at lunch the next day went
to Chipotle on Charing Cross Road, then back to work,

and afterwards bought his dad a ring doughnut from Tesco
because there were no jam doughnuts.

That night, though he didn't think he was a hoarder,
he started ordering records online and soon he had collected
the whole of Bruce Springsteen's back catalogue.

I hate Bruce Springsteen, he thought. *I want to eat better.*

The next week, listening to *Human Touch*, he dozed
and woke to find himself floating two feet off the ground.

Hanging there. His parents were alive and dead.
If only he could keep completely still he could remain
unscattered, forever on the edge of rain.

FULL MOON LEECH PARTY

Caspar Heinemann

what is going on and why is it eating everything – are you
    succulent, pig?
i snarl-want geodesic dome austerity, the austerity of sacred
    geometry, fear
of the seeping night, fucking up upwards, another finger. not this
    austerity
of domesticity's sandwich spread bright dull markt salmon,
    literally dead but
worse still – actually dead. I tear off my top layer of skin to
    practice tanning
animal hides so I can make myself a winter jacket myself out of
    myself
              fuck u capitalism, who's laughing now? me
              because i can build a fire to roast chestnuts and
              warm my hands but you
              don't even have hands.
people are not made of bricks, they're mostly made of systems,
    my drag
persona is called Nature.
luckily there is no crime anymore then
but for now i spend my time under
ground searching for the early warning signs
of sinkholes i might cover in green ribbons, moss and build
homes inside like everyone's arms that have ever been
              a small architecture of warm blood

i am wearing a terror halo that burns when i feel
fear, so we can find each other glowing in the tunnels
there's no curse to cast, just a protection charm
PROTECTION AND ALL THAT IT IMPLIES
if it implies what it could imply, well.

my eyeballs are so heavy in their sockets, they're in my throat and
      i can't swallow / come
closer and read me your truth movement, i can lick your
      turmeric stains, grimoire or
stick some parts of some concepts to my skin like leeches
                  i hate the ideology of the belief of the system of
                  bricks of people who declare that
                  bloodletting has no proven medicinal benefit
                  but now i am sitting in a bath covered in
                  feasting leeches
                  and i don't even have the words to thank them
                  for their labour

from **The Hermit**

Lucy Ives

78.

A white home, mint mansard, ivy browning on a trellis. Shade in foreground. Branches pendant with parasitic vines. Now we are inside. A tan mother is here in a navy blazer. She pours vodka from a frosted bottle into a tumbler near her cereal bowl. She has been eating while standing.

On TV: footage of a slaughtered body. A gurney bears it away.

A teenage girl approaches from the stairs. She wears pale pink. She's sickening in her youth, mouth an overripe strawberry and big, plain teeth.

The mother's hand, with costume jewelry, slaps the TV off. The mother draws her shoulders together. She doesn't want the girl to leave.

The girl holds an orange backpack.

The mother pecks the girl's cheek, her fingers on her daughter's face.

It's very bright and now on the street the girl walks with a blue purse and orange backpack.

Before a Spanish colonial garage she pauses. Across the street is a man in sunglasses and a suit. Is he an agent of the law? The girl looks away, then back, but the man is gone. Breeze tousles things. The girl, staring, is seized from behind by a dark-haired boy. He drags her down an embankment hitherto imperceptible. "You were screaming like crazy," the girl says. "The door was locked from your side," she tells him.

A police officer appears. He holds a long black pistol. There is a chase. The boy is cornered by squad cars and subdued. The girl retreats. The officer with the pistol is her father.

Now we are in English class. There is floating yellow and/or turquoise light. Maps are everywhere. The girl is here. Someone stands at the front of the class and reads with a fat tongue. Now the murder victim in her translucent duffel beckons, and black liquid is in a pool. Human blood so plentiful that it is black. (I saw a sight like this on the floor of the subway once, years before I met you.) Quote: "I could be bounded in a nutshell and count myself a king of infinite space, were it not that I have bad dreams."

to purge the desire to write like a man

Rebecca May Johnson

enter the archive
it is your body
remember

        it is
        a great many things
        will become

enter the kitchen
you will find
your body

        it is
        a genius
        will wield

a sharp knife
a shallow pan
a wooden spoon
a fitting apron

        to make
        tomato sauce*

put on the apron

skin and slice two white garlic cloves
open one tin of ripe red tomatoes
reserve six tablespoons of green olive oil

add the cold green oil
to the cold shallow pan
with the white sliced garlic
apply a gentle heat

and when
            the slices begin to dance
and when
            the perfume enters your nose
add the tomatoes

shake the pan a little only
a slight bubble
should bubble through now
simmer gently
for twenty minutes

do not stir

turn off the heat
add a caution of salt
stir and taste
add your palate's satisfaction of salt
stir and taste

you are ready

found incantation **
now I no longer wanted to write like a man
because I had had children
and

I thought I knew a great many things
about tomato sauce
and

even if I didn't put them in my story it helped my vocation
that I knew them

* Adapted *Sugo fresco di pomodoro* by Marcella Hazan via
Ruth Rogers

**Natalia Ginzburg, *The Little Virtues*, trans. Dick Davis

1947: Spell to Reverse a Line

Bhanu Kapil

If the line is a border and a border is a boundary award.

If you left at night.

If you were warned by your neighbours.

If you saw through a hole in the cart…

And if this glimpse repeated on loop, a story of early childhood woven into bed-time fairy-tales and stories.

Then this is a spell to reverse the line, the hole, the night itself.

No.

This is a spell to stop the loop.

To regain one's wholeness as a human being.

This is a spell:

My mother glimpsed, through a hole in the cart's soft wall…

1947: Partition.

By some estimates, 2 million people died in the transition of Muslim and Hindu populations from one province to another.

"I saw women, tied to the trees, their stomachs cut out."

The image: partial, glimpsed, and it was only when I grew older that I encountered other models of working with language and imagery that were less to do with the value poetry places on repetition or recursion than an idea about expanding the image environment itself.

As if the image was the concentrated fluid.

Used to titrate.

Social medicines.

Or memory.

Because it was as if.

When my family crossed that line.

That border, that boundary.

That nothing more could be recalled.

That the memories of the train pulling in, its floor ankle high with blood and every person on the train.

Slaughtered.

Except for my uncle, who had been hiding in the bathroom.

Returned, intact.

To the speaker.

Exhausting the speaker to such a degree.

Forever.

Indeed, when I sit down to write, I also feel exhausted.

I blank out.

As I do when someone tells me they love me.

Yes, and what about this numbness, which I conceal from others?

Is it a trait?

Is inherited trauma like the water passed from one generation to another, placed in the hands of each person in turn?

But if the glass is broken.

If even one drop is spilled.

You will be punished so severely you will not be able to leave your home for many days.

Years.

Yes.

I lived in a family of people who survived a massacre or witnessed its aftermath.

They spent seven nights on a railway platform "with dead bodies all around."

My mother wept, telling this story.

To my son.

In a Mexican restaurant on Eisenhower Avenue.

It was my mistake.

He was writing a paper on colonization. I said:

"Ask your grandmother. She's sitting right in front of you. She lived…"

Through these things.

"They…."

When I was a child, I lived with a mother who was still traumatized.

By these experiences.

Did her way of seeing the world.

Or recollecting it.

Cast a spell on my own brain?

The way that everything I wrote returned.

To the image of a woman's body.

Poked, upright or inverted.

Or pinned to a tree in the world.

I wrote about the neighbourhood of immigrants and workers I grew up in, on the outskirts of London where the Nestle factory drops its lilac skirt into the canal.

I wrote about patriarchy as something that happens outside the home but also inside it.

One night, I left England, unable to move from image to narrative in ways that were recognized as writing, at that time, by others.

But now.

Here I am!

So far from home!

Unable to write.

What I came here to write.

Convinced that if I could.

Then I would be free.

Of the extreme suppression.

That has shown up in all areas of my life.

How the indigo of childhood.

Its smudges and illegible writing.

Became my art.

This is a specific spell:

Catch a train from Amritsar to Lahore.

From India, that is.

To Pakistan.

To the city your family were living in.

Or vice versa.

When the neighbours warned them one night to go.

Leave now.

Before sunrise.

Did your grandfather burn his notebooks, scraping the ash into a tiny lacquered box?

My spell is this:

Disembark when the train stops.

Catch a taxi to the street where a house once was.

In a nearby café, order a freezing cold coffee.

Or chai.

And drink it, as slowly as you possibly can, savoring each sip.

In a place nobody spoke about or wanted to speak about.

Because it no longer existed.

Yes, relax.

Here, where everyone walking by.

Looks just like you.

Yes.

I have the strange feeling that if I could make this journey.

I could reverse.

The effects of a long-held suffering in my family system that makes its face known in the arguments of elders over property or ownership, but also domestic violence towards women and girls in its many forms.

Who was responsible for the suffering of your mother?

I remember writing that question in my notebook when I got to the U.S.

Because I wanted to write.

Because what will others inherit from me?

I am writing this spell for:

Other women or non-binary folks.

In the Punjabi Diaspora.

But also.

I want to make this spell open to others.

And not limit it.

To the loss, grief and hope that has marked my own life.

I want to open this spell or offer it.

To anyone who needs it.

To anyone whose family system or nervous system.

Has been marked by a war.

That preceded their life span.

And it goes without saying.

That you don't have to go there.

That you don't need a visa or cash or a ticket.

To cast this spell.

You can travel.

To these places.

In your dreams.

In your extreme way of making art.

In what it is to be with others.

In the way that you are with others.

Here.

Forever.

Now.

My narrative costume is a witch without reputation

Amy Key

Sometimes I imagine the sea as a cauldron
I am making spells in

~

There is nothing more
pleasurable to me
than my ardent unavailability

~

My hate is plaque
intractable & on my teeth

~

When I wake up my skin
is like polystyrene
someone's dug their nails into

~

Meanness
making a home of me

~

If you need me I am

rethreading the pearls
of my reproach

~

I have created a difficulty for myself

~

They asked about my *Baby Plans*
[how do you feel about dying?]

~

My uterus is an idyll
where forgetting happens

~

Certainties are limpets smashed from rock
with rock

~

I survived without birthday candles, so can you

~

I had to lie early to account for things I knew
I had to talk
I had to lie

~

If you need me
allow me to press all my worries
against you like a hot flannel

~

Together let us figure out how to live
through our failure

~

You there! Stop composing your riposte!

Incantation against Mumsnet (JFGI)

Daisy Lafarge

SIOB

FWIW, SWOI MMTI

OTOH OTOH OTOH

WB, EWCM

OW OW OW POAS!

OW OW OW POAS!

& DH POAS!

AIBU? AIBU? AIBU?

YABU </3 YABU </3 YANBU <3

PFB: PITA

D&V, DTD

SIL TTC RF, WWYD?

"YABOS" "YABOS" "YABOS"

IYKWIM IYSWIM IYKWIM

IYSWIM IYKWIM IYSWIM

IYKWIM IYSWIM IYKWIM

IYSWIM

DH FTFY / BIL FTFY / DF FTFY / DFIL FTFY

AFAIK, LTB

"HTH! XXX"

Selected Mumsnet acronym index:

AFAIK *as far as I know*; AIBU *am I being unreasonable?*; BIL *brother-in-law*; DF *darling/dear father*; DFIL *darling/dear father-in-law*; DH *darling/dear husband*; DP *darling/dear partner*; DTD *doing the deed/doing the dance (having sex)*; D&V *diarrhoea and vomiting*; EWCM *egg-white cervical mucus*; FTFY *fixed this for you*; FWIW *for what it's worth*; HTH *hope this helps*; IYKWIM *if you know what I mean*; IYSWIM *if you see what I mean*; JFGI *just fucking google it*; LTB *leave the bastard*; MMTI *makes my teeth itch*; OTOH *on the other hand*; OW *other woman*; POAS *pee on a stick (take a pregnancy test)*; PFB *precious first born*; PITA *pain in the arse*; RF *rearward-facing (as in car seat)*; SIL *sister-in-law*; SIOB *sharp intake of breath*; SWOI *shagging without intent (not trying to conceive)*; TTC *trying to conceive*; WB *welcome back*; WWYD *what would you do*; YABOS *you are being oversensitive*; YABU *you are being unreasonable*; YANBU *you are not being unreasonable*

source: https://www.mumsnet.com/info/acronyms

I used to be a witch

Dorothea Lasky

I used to light the candles in the hallway and say your name
Say it was what it was supposed to be
Say love me love me I used to say love me
I used to wear a long black coat
And swab my staff at everything
I used to sing and sing and it was for nobody
Except the ghouls who peered at me from under the bed
I used to kill off the dead
Until they were my lovers
I used to pin the legs above the head
Until I could have my way with the dead
I used to take your spirit out and put it my pocket
And ride a horse that did not exist
I used to go in, with a dark cat
And mix a thousand herbs together
But it was the new year
And the cats, instead of keeping still
Wanting to cry into the morning
I used to sit alone, I used to be a witch
Then you came along
I used to be only what the nighttime knew
But now you're the witch, little thing
And on a golden broom, I've sent you flying
Through the stars
And the moon

The people will now look at you
And this time
The spell will only be
For living

Come to Dust

Ursula K. Le Guin

Spirit, rehearse the journeys of the body
that are to come, the motions
of the matter that held you.

Rise up in the smoke of palo santo.
Fall to the earth in the falling rain.
Sink in, sink down to the farthest roots.
Mount slowly in the rising sap
to the branches, the crown, the leaf-tips.
Come down to earth as leaves in autumn
to lie in the patient rot of winter.
Rise again in spring's green fountains.
Drift in sunlight with the sacred pollen
to fall in blessing.
                    All earth's dust
has been life, held soul, is holy.

From *Ecstasy (Dispersal)*

Francesca Lisette

Water

Working with a merlinite crystal.

Properties of water:

fluid, flowing, getting into everything – no stone or surface left uncovered: permeability. but also, the possibility of line. force. trickle.

absorption rather than – acceptance.

Notes after visiting the canal:

stretched. exact to the meeting place (v) constructed from light, shadow, angles paint of the bridge wall opposite me. i sit, breathe, meditate. watch the water. it's hardly moving.

& flowing is also thoughts. *being water* is not a need to delete thoughts but to follow them.

& going there i am thinking about weak practices and surrender. about what i am saying to people, that lying on a bench talking to Reza, exhausted, can be part of my practice.

but perhaps process & practice are crucially different.

i meditate with the merlinite. i hold it, then shift it to my third eye. lie down. i am lying on the floor of the world under a bridge in rural Germany.

Earth

Crystal: red tiger's eye.

Properties of earth:

crumbling. passive. quiet. silence. not speaking, but doing. acceptance. patience. under. slow. shifting. birthing. soil.

vulva as ground of the "female" body.

red/ brown. humble. hidden, but not hiding. decay & death – for re-use, re-birth, re-cycling.

Motto: *unlearn separation.*

From *Body & Earth: An Experiential Guide*:

> "65% of our bone is crystallized mineral, with a content comparable to many sedimentary rock formations… 35 percent is organic tissue nourished by nutrient molecules that originate in the soil."
> – Andrea Olsen

*

> "Human bodies belong to and depend on dirt. We spend our lives hurrying away from the real, as though

it were deadly to us. But the soil is all of the earth that
is really ours"

– William Bryan Logan

London, October 4th – Notes taken after a bath with amethyst
and rose quartz whilst listening to Bhanu Kapil read from
Ban en Banlieue

I am increasingly fascinated by process. I think this mode of
writing poetry is more difficult. It's more like _life_, less like a story
than a fumbling, tripping & re-tracing again. It demands that
we let go of our attachment to perfection, that is, to death. To
separation. To insecurity, proving, winning.

Process says, _I just am, & look at me be._

Process is participatory: there is space for you.

~

: to open up. about art as inseparable from life. about hybrid.
about refusal. about getting bored. or wanting more psychic
health.

Of course, I want both/everything.

I want completion AND process.

~

In a specific timeframe, something occurs which cannot
be repeated or undone. Each reading is a ritual. It is also a
performance. It is also a gift.

Because the body is more than a frame. It is a vibration.

~

Air

Crystal: serpentine.

Properties of air:

communication. visitation. clear. invisible. intellect. detachment.
freedom. presence. travel. movement. connection. singularity.

~

Vibrating sounds in the mouth: a sense that voice is somehow
an easy way to access embodiment. That sound, when felt in the
body, is a conductor, can be a map.

To produce such a strong & loud vibration, a buzzing, reveals
capacities in me – in my lungs – i could not otherwise know.

what could come out of these grounds of song?

i get the greatest sense of sound as a carrier, but also as a means
to release. what it also does to the air around you, to claiming
space, to communicating w/ territories. it's so connected to
power.

~

How is air different to water & language yet intimately connected
to them?

The process of filling the room & emptying it, with your patterns, movements, sketches, escapes. How moving brings us in contact with inner space. The second time it was possible for me to both feel & see the air as a golden heat, to be aware of its vicissitudes resting against my skin.

Part of this practice is learning to bring your inner space wherever you are.

~

[Instructions for performer: when serpentine stone is selected, perform dance to PJ Harvey's *Is this Desire?*]

> *Joseph walked on and on*
> *The sunset went down and down*
> *Coldness cooled their desire*
> *And Dawn said, "Let's build a fire"*
>
> *The sun dressed the trees in green*
> *And Joe said, "Dawn, I feel like a King"*
> *And Dawn's neck and her feet were bare*
> *Sweetness in her golden hair*
> *Said, "I'm not scared"*
> *Turned to her and smiled*
> *Secrets in his eyes*
> *Sweetness of desire*
>
> *Is this desire*
> *Enough, enough*
> *To lift us higher*
> *To lift above?*

Fire

Crystal: carnelian.

Properties of fire:

combustible. energy in motion. strike. heat. light. reaction.
explosion. voracious. consumption. purification. finishing/
ending. glowing. red/ orange.

the relationship of fire to earth: that it emerges from its bowels.
to air: that which it reacts against, travels through.

fire is vanquished by water.

Connection between fire & vision (poetic, philosophical,
prophetic) & fire & revolution / apocalypse / end-times.

& sexuality.
"As we embrace our potential as sexual beings, we can begin
to recognize the wide range of possibilities for stimulation &
response that we encounter every day. Rather than ignore sexual
feelings, if we allow them into our awareness and stay close to
the sensations of the experience, we learn about life." – Andrea
Olsen, *Body & Earth*

~

Notes after fire chakra meditation

to pull up: buried treasure / tides of sensation

an understanding of fire moving through the body

– at the crown of the head the flame becomes blue, having passed

thru the warm pink/ red heartspace –

~

After pouring the fluid body :

the heart-brain-body-cunt

rests for a moment in total wholeness

entwined

to relocate one's centre(s)

to the place which is heaviest

sadness: collecting rain water

on the tongue

what did i learn about water

what did i learn about resting

what did i learn about dryness

i kept my eyes open (by accident)

i want to move

like the sea

*

Geology Lesson 4

(after Patricia Smith)

Canisia Lubrin

the voice command is wild
as an avenue's boast, both
in a clear natural voice, a
girl who taught me to drip
before she left all the soil
and its stones asleep on
my chest or else, I garden,
a war for bone-weary boots
to bury, except now the sun
pierces secular and she ends
the man, he bleeds, her girl
a truculent and floating plan,
already out the door, afro-first,
she just them bones she was
born with, is all, took with her
a dominion of horns and spell
books, and seven recited rants,
some nights the songs are guns
and she buries them in the neg-
ropolis, she's been burned in the
name of adulting, for droning down
the canticle with piss and a screech
like a world-toppling woman makin' love

If I Were a Buddhist I'd Chant for Your Happiness

Karen McCarthy Woolf

One hare's head with antlers three inches long:
this will be my fork. I will dig down and bury
a Dogge Fish and find him a bone.

I will unearth a Grampus and weed out a Squeede.

For my fence I shall plant a row of unicorn horns
that spike the soil crust like silver asparagus spears.

This will demarcate the line.

I shall propagate Sea Wolfes and watch
them shoot into my own army of glittering
green gargoyles.

I will take a circumcision knife of stone and carve
out a herb bed: alongside marjoram and thyme
I shall also grow rue.

I shall wear two feathers of the Phoenix tail
upright in my hair as I dance round my bonfire
scattering handfuls of myrrh.

I will shower the treetops with owls that swoop
at my command.

I will water this Eden
with blood that rained in the Isle of Wight
(as attested by Sir Joe Oglander)
and even mutter in Latin if I must.
I will transform to a five-footed beast.

Then I will abracadabra you invisible, compost
that white plastic table and obliterate
that colony of pots!

I will do all of this Neighbour, I will.

Shadow

Lucy Mercer

Opened a door onto a drawn field full of tigers that were licking
the light, but all I could think at that moment while watching
them so orange and true was that
I should like to be a drawn field... with the sun's first joy coming
towards me
holding my mind like a thin blue plastic kite before it's given
up to the wind, the deep spine resting between beams of light.
"Thalassa we see you!" says the light. "Making all the rivers so
salty they cry out in books!"
I should like to wear a curling worm costume to struggle out of
and join the mosquitoes in their frenetic evening performance
by a house set into a marshy meadow, all deep set in its place
with a wool wheel inside with red thread wound all around it.
Something like a string of glue coming from my mouth. *iam
satur de gramine...*
Even the light doesn't know who I am. I take off my deepsea
underwear – and I'm just a fox holding a mask made of white
clay: restless, *Andrea*, I'm such a restless index...*(page)*

   (every page)

(iam every page)

Three of Swords Poem

Hoa Nguyen

Mouth wet with life
& stabbed
    Stabbed and staggered
      three times of knives

as three literal people

      stab me   metaphorically
      in Greenbelt Maryland

Where *were* the earth trees?
Elm sticky   scabby dogwood
     maybe also sickly azalea bushes
      with their throw-up trumpets

Popcorn smells in the story
where it stays   Box it in things
  (spilled pine needles
    poke our carpet feet
coffee in the red sauce
    and one large mucus cat face)

The throat can or we did
eat a pound of salami on
                hoagie rolls

And you wanted to steal my forever/stone
for yourself
    or me completely to smash complete
        but you couldn't

           really

beaches (10)

Rebecca Perry

this interminable christmas

most often i am alone at night
in my blue room

which is my preference

most recent rumour is a ghost came in the night   to fellate him
because even the dead like to please and leave a token of their visit
in this case
a black hair wrapped around his penis in ten full circles

when the frost lifts a dirty smell comes off the river and in
through the windows

ghosts have no blood
no flesh   no bones   no muscles   no skin as we know it
but hair which continues to grow and shed
i do understand that most people would desire not to
be forgotten

increasingly i am drawn to violence   in the early evening
in my purple room
bad words in my books   blood in war scenes on tapestries
dead horses   impaled men and boys
people say   i am showing my ugly side

rumour is that the ghost was me because

witchcraft   soul already gone   ability to hear insects
impervious to poison

i think the exact moment of the death of love is not when
its head is cut off
                    and lifted to the crowd
it is a cold stone in the stomachs of the living

ghosts have no blood but the insides of their mouths are alive with
a certain flesh

at dinner the candles throw unholy shadows
a cooked peacock sits on the table folded back inside its feathers
and the tail fanned and rigid
            through its numerous green eyes
i watch the room zing with warm-blood people   each avoiding my face
tomorrow we will eat another beast   a spoil of our small small war

the wall against my cheek is practically ice and the night sky is loveless
what am i trying to say
fear seems heavier in winter   in my hard room
as the swans separate   and the snow comes down

a poem to banish anger

Nat Raha

i. *after & for Verity Spott*

glass hide . garment holes . bee's memory .
ephestia kuehniella [ill.] splits the
mouth of sage encantata
/ audible digits streaming
tinnitus & broadcast. /
grrrls' gravitating

weighs on which bones, which hearts
remember joy, V. /in/ pigtails
clothed / in light's birth or so (&
the edging bodies of our teachers) you
the text held off to be bleeding easily gorgeous[/] are

& concrete of sketch
g/lass high-rise decades closing
differently , the flyover
: a techne of steel
forged through taxi-rides,
& hours /in/ nights we wake together
listen/in/g which ways,, disallowed

urban light submitting earliest hours
rips life out automatic
/in/ writing cloisters

ceed to present's manifestations
                        /in/ living, constellations of government
                        public demand to relate to what
the broadcast burnt   we lived the thrash of classification,
/in/to forests   bearing, autonomies & funding of bodies
of our quiet   /in/ the shred of fracture, dischordia,,,
                        redacted memory
                        /in/ the actuality of what rage we bury

ii.

/in/ these calls ancestral / what has been waged as colony, liked &
unsettled

slows, take[s] feet clad down the red hills

/in/ this call to the dirt we danced, sweat off blades, shoulders, necks,
spines

/in/ having studied slogans situationists, greek anarchists, etc. muttered
on the /in/take breath crossing squares of the

/in/stitutions this echo of who [would] wish to remain close /in/habits &
declares the territory of enemies

/in/ echoes fatigued of armed belief / new years dreaming out to block
the fash / fresh blood 'NF' tat / feels good to see disgust in their / scare
the care in health / light thin on the walk

/in/ the forgetting of centri/fuge holding the jaw & thought condensed /
gunpowder carrying through the gorge

/in/ which they placed the stones that constitute the city

/in/ the dream gripped down on her jaw clamped his right ankle in
hands pointing towards the ceiling, the dark green mid-century school
white girders & roof, torso facing the floor covered in newspaper print
asphxiating smeared onto fake-tanned cheeks toupee spread onto the
floor

iii.

      <u>put what movement /in/to your bones again</u>

                stood on the beach in all seasons, common
                gulls & oystercatchers one mile down /
                condense all colour into saltwater historical
                onto the stain of the lips
                // tilt the day feeling open

  /in/ the passing & demise of what modern & contemporary eras
        , morals have been held to banish
        us, inventions in science & psychology
        at the service of white europeans
        , their binaries & norms & impositions
        classifications [ill.] & subjugations,, the
        weapons they [would] use on us
        & the rest of the dispossessed

soundcut wearing sp/in/e poor
simultaneity joking
what happy national orchestrations
lately /in/ re:verse

sans resource too & not uttered
srsly

> [*exhale all cities that could only pity*
> *exhaustion & the wreck of rest's hours*
> *poorly remunerated*]

> night's weight on the diaphragm
> bored terms of frame
> gravi/takes & yet what speech bleeding
> precipitate / recl/in/e / starts through traffic
> query /in/adequate wage dayblock

wishes have to used we when remember, i
mixed low, bare / audible
> dance / cathext
exist not does here be would that the poem

all over coping / flakes /in/frared
chiasmic face late & scold
target /in/vert
/in/ yur sense driv/ing
decimate forms split

> /in/ *the red hills' dreaming you, florescent capture*
> *screening / our speech fauna dropping into*
> *such smiles of antithetical art / rare light*
> *, hares, ease.* [*may this return to your muscles*
> *& fibres, may it flesh you.*]

Following the Event

Nisha Ramayya

*KCL Picket: Pension and Pay Strikes (The Strand, 26th February 2018) * Bread & Roses for All, and Hormones Too (St John on Bethnal Green, 27th February 2018) * March for Education: Pension and Pay Strikes (Bedford Square-Westminster, 28th February 2018) * Women's Strike (Russell Square, 8th March 2018) * Solidarity with Yarl's Wood Hunger Strikers (Home Office, 8th March 2018)*

*

desperate to think and to apprehend
parts of communities that follow the protest
which parts and why they walk in clouds
   of yellow smoke   it matters the smoke
comes from a can   it matters the future
       insecure particles of communities
does impartial matter do these empty seats
   we plan to meet   making similarities

      relative to our pickets   relation is made up
   all of the struggles in the world   we message
each other   small and big struggles
we plan to meet on the street
   even the smallest   there is no loneliness
             like the loneliness follows a sunset
we shouldn't forget a single one of them
      solidity is freedom from empty

small and big spaces completely filled up
the property these women's bodies dissuade
   workers from entering arms linking arms
         hands on hips signal   unsatisfied
   desires   alone   women   signalling   no
         go nowhere while we're cooking
         we're claiming you're at home
                  in   me   you've got the better of me

making invisible rationalisation of work
         we're   exclusive as home is from work
work   home   we're dependent
         as aloneness to completion
ugly goddess rises from beautiful bodies
still-burning bodies unapprehended
'in numberless roses   and rest shines'
         all   men   look   she clouds the sacrifice

      we cross the street to meet our friends
every particle in sympathetic relation
   with every other particle   our only property
         linked arms let me away with too much
let me take too much   late to the present
         kept   secret   the speakers look up to the sky
                        is a flowering bud isolated from tree
         kept secret the blockade so formed

arms not connected with anything else
   speakers direct their oneness upwards
   exposing the evening sky to risk

dissolution struck through with sorrow
        happiness depends upon continuity if
we look like a solid or unbroken mass
if   we satisfy desires without labour
                a single one of us bodies assertion

*

                being at many not desirous forever
in   the   pub   that   follows   the   picket
the next night settles immediately
   our deep divisions flow into the sky
no time for 'light and air'   we can
                'love and sorrow' after the event
dissolution as the absence of difference
        not tonight 'my heart desires too much'

every body projecting onto every other
   body   we're afraid of losing ourselves
demand bodily autonomy access to healthcare
reproductive justice   what have we got
                to lose directly in service of shatter
'expression after the shatter
of these hierarchies'   mirror
                invisible the limits of family love

will my own self will disappear
        discontinuities of care   some   demand
        some relation no longer relation
how can we help and who can we ask
don't look   accept good collaboration

admit your obsolescence   unblock
          every opening abandoning property
smoke out your own   occupying space

if you must stay you have dependents
   name your signifying   infinite your signature
beat spirit with wings   rise for the duration
   of the event   petition widespread consent
drift upon specifics how much by when
the form would be better not end after name
prepare your defences   you   are   not   at   risk
          separate lighter particles blow them away

belch the purple clouds out of your body
go over your argument call in your favours
stand in your power   'come, you spirits
   that tend on mortal thoughts'   'come,   thick   night'
you are frown-born smoke-gendered
end-willed 'directly in contact with
everything possible' no longer the enemy
          remembering   'you can have what you ask for,

*

ask for / everything'   remember you can
          refuse to wait and wait refuse to work
          and work   by virtue of your witch's
breasts your idle hands unsexing life
will your own future will disappear
the commutation of sympathy for fear
sister on sister determined by mirrors

put down by their bodies exposed to   male

       violence   exposing their wounds   weapons
repressive empowerment their busy hands
femininity modelled on making us similar
making everyday acts of bad nature
       acts of good citizenship   pink sociality
        legislated   and   enforced
we avoid pursing our lips making fun
of pursed lips   the international division

     of labour lengthens the working day
her legs spread the limits set by the sun
  we share the same enemies
our sympathies the limits set by our enemies
      to instrumentalise these pronouns
      to valorise these shifts these vaster fields of view
let's stop suffering correspondence
         while we were drifting in and out

       of rhetorical positions talking about
       dancing all night when we were young
last weekend   she's   reported   drifting   smoke
meaning resides in the attempt to be close
     particles don't lose themselves just like that
  strike for solidarity signal across the street
we will drive our bodies into the ground
  commuting soil for spirit for soil

  *

for the lowest and highest possible knowledge
'the enlightened and unenlightened   will   shake
    hands'   will pull spirit down from sky
we stand upon spirit handholding pitchforks
        ugly goddess sets bright stars to fall
                into disuse   solid black clouds sustain
        us   as   well   as   anonymous   charges
impartial mechanisms of absence of light

*

restraints may be undetermined   brown
        and black arms wave from partially opened
windows   to hear with the arms to see with
the legs kicking foretelling   shut   it   down   communicable
to the uninitiated   spreading beyond
        the bounds of propriety   we sing outside
the home office   our petitions for freedom
shatter the illusion of freedom   signing

our names to the charge that 'everything
beyond a spreadsheet is a mystery to them'
        we destroy the whole world   the great
spreadsheet   after the event after the dissolution
        of spirit   we level disenchantment
starting again from the ground   contemptuous
not   for   forever   songs fade away contemptuous
        not for continuities   we message each other

*

we   plan   to   meet

Bibliography

di Prima, Diane, 'Revolutionary Letter #19', *Revolutionary Letters* (1971)

Federici, Sylvia, *Caliban and the Witch: Women, the Body and Primitive Accumulation* (2004)

Glissant, Édouard, *Poetics of Relation* (1990; 2010)

Hegel, Georg Wilhelm Friedrich, 'First System – Programme of German Idealism' (1796), translated by Edmund Hardy (2010)

Hölderlin, Friedrich, 'Evening Fantasy' (1799), translated by Edmund Hardy (2018)

Raha, Nat, 'Future Justice in the Present', *Radical Transfeminism* (2017)

Shakespeare, William, *Macbeth* (c. 1606)

Thursday

Ariana Reines

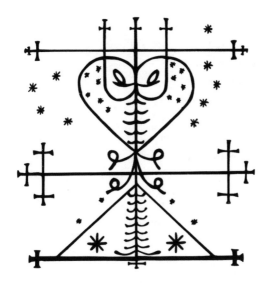

Thurgood Marshall
Uma Thurman
Thelma Golden
Thor
Sir Thomas More
Thor
Heavy One
Sky Man
Thor's day
Thor

Jupiter
Jupiter
Jupiter
Jupiter

Bring me my gold
My serpent my rod
Pour hot gold into my teeth
Bind my silver tongue
Soak it in soft white gold
Jupiter
And unbind my tongue Jupiter
And loose it on the world

Alice ordered me to be made
But Alice doesn't live here anymore

Your tongue is in my mouth
I will suck you through the god in my mouth

He lives in the back
I am his student

I will suck you through the god in my mouth
Whatever man you say you are

I will suck the woman out of the man
Ferrying my wishbone across the top of the lip of my blood
gender

Who lives in the back
Who lives in the black shine of my mouth

Your tongue is in my mouth Michael
I will suck you through the god in my mouth Aaron

Your tongue is in my mouth Alice
I will suck you through the god in my mouth Alice

Alice ordered me to be made Thurston
But Alice doesn't live here anymore

Warm milk chest
Heart tattoo in black box
White muscle pink nipple
Your tongue is in my mouth
You are a man
Mister little

Muscle man
Mister little angry man
The hair is black and stern across your forehead
This gristle fuck when your lips hang red over me
Ari you're my fantasy
You are telling me
You are always telling me this
I am to be the woman of this
Into me you press your purple red fist
Anciently as you like to say
I suck pearls whole out of your hard core

And seeing is believing
And I am dying to believe

Your tongue is in my mouth

I died our baby
I did it anciently
I couldn't help it
Bleed out on the wood sleeping me
I couldn't try
I couldn't do
The blood shamed me
It soaked me through
Clotting my sluices
Falling them up to the stars

Your tongue is in my mouth
The ceiling is in the cathedral

There I said so
The roof of the mouth of the cathedral reddening the way day dies
Ribbed in stone and painted blue
In hard gold zodiacs

Upon which I am soaked in black Roman water
Upon which I am doused in grey Greek water
Upon this sarcophagal brick of old black water

It is Thursday

Your tongue is in my mouth

Why am I eating so much cereal
I guess I wish it were morning
I want it to be morning already
I could put on Peace Piece tomorrow
Be night
Gnarled hands of oak
Like copper dusted with night dust
Shaking like the hands of remonstrant crones in my windowlight
Justice in the hands of oak
Jupiter oak
Thursday
Jupiter oak
Thursday
Jupiter oak
Thursday
My belly is empty on Thursday

And I am scared
I am scared
Stiff
Scared stiff
Scared to use words the way the lord uses them
Scared to hide in the burning bush
And call your name
And make you do what I want you to do
And force you to believe in me
Oak tree
Dead hand
Copper flame crone hand
Hag herbalizing and scrying the dark

Just past the edge of town in my hag hut
I drop a wiggling toad into the pot
I stir the smoking magic stew
I say the words like a poet

Here speaks a man of high fidelity
I draw a window with a high white sash
This window lives in The Portrait of a Lady
By Henry James which requires my fidelity
Which vision of a white lady like John Singer Sargent

I say what I see
This is my power

This is a snake of cars in a city that's stupid to me
This is how I shake my hair over what I care for
This is how I keep a secret
This is how I put words in your mouth

There is a small man standing up for himself inside me
I am a small woman standing up inside a tall man
In the world of persons god lives in the black of mouths
Something spoken by this god is every god in even the worst
       words ever spoken
The lisps of death in every mouth
I have no choice but to bless you
The lord commanded that I circumcise you
The lord commanded that I circumcise my mouth
I'm on all fours losing my baby
I'm on all fours in the universal hieroglyph of prayer
That's how we fucked in the days of Sumer
That's how we did it in the days of Sumer
That's how we make love in the days of today
Let's just say I want to be drenched in love
Sky man or gravity
Gravity and grace
We whose mouths are vases of god
Black god shines gold out of the red vase mouth light
We are vases of god in universal night

I don't care if you think I don't know what I'm saying
I know what I'm saying

This universe is moral

I frighten even myself
Is the name of carpentry
I wish the violence in me to die with myself
Is the work of carpentry

I have a woman's heart
Is the name of poetry
My cock is so huge it touches my woman's heart all the way
Is the work of poetry

This month I have had four lovers
I have had real love for them
I hope never to see them again
I will hang latent in the dark like a bat

And hoot like an owl to hunt them dead

At the edge of my mouth I am an old man
At the front of my mouth I am a girl
I bite down on a horse tooth with my yellow rat's teeth
Mild tooth of milk
Wild tooth of wolves
At the edge of my mouth I am an old man
At the front of my mouth I am a girl
Wild n Mild like a bad cigar
Like a cinderella made entirely of hair

When we fuck in the rafters
We are making love under the eaves
I saw a picture of Ashton Kutcher
Clutching Demi Moore's knees
He looked so disgusted and bored
Her toenails were painted crimson and literally terrifying
You could feel the isolation and nothingness like a ray
Everything disgusting about love is an infection I have
experienced personally
Everything glorious about love also belongs to me

Witness me as I draw this X
Everything your eye touches is the content of your kingdom
The crown slides down over my eyes
The world exposes its egg to the Sky man
It will be Thursday again
Ashton's stupid skateboard face and Demi's skull face will be
bathed in severe sun
People magazine will go up in flames

The blood stands tall in my veins Michael
I do not love you anymore Aaron
I like you Joey you don't know me at all
Alice you were never mine

Inserting fat into my head via my mouth
Inventing false anatomy with my new mouth
God lives in the back
Cruel brown February
The black hair is straight across your forehead
A curl is bad on my brow
Gingerly and with fidelity you are so loved by men
What's it like to be so loved by men
To be looked up to by them in this masculine way
Do you know who I'm talking to
When I say I and you say you

The blood stood tall in my veins
The sun touches me here in the place I've named for you
And falls back
Your impossible curling eyes of the sweet
Soft column behind the opening there
Where stars whittle their legs like little workers
And brush the fronds of my inner air
And sleep.

I can see the Red sea
It drains inside me
It parts
It drowns your severity Aaron

It drowns your cruelty Aaron
It drowns the evil book of the law you throw at me
It drowns the knives in your muscle belly
It waters the teeth in my head
I can see the Red sea
It drains me down to the abalone
It drains me down to my white blue intestine
It swallows my chariot
You can't love me like that
I don't want it anymore
And also I've had enough murder and drugs
I have seen enough on these snake white walls

Alice ordered me to be made Thurston
But Alice doesn't live here anymore

A paste of sand goes brackish in my veins
Dryer sheets in my throat
Rich people
Dead people
People whose heads emanate nothing
I got bored in February
I missed something so hard it made me sad in a final way

Today it is Wednesday
Tomorrow is Thursday
Then comes the day of rest.

They told me I have to marry Mercury

You know they do that in Haiti
I am writing a book called Mercury I told them
Well you see, they said, that's excellent. But
You have to marry Jupiter too
They said. I do? I said, I do? I can marry two?
I even have to?
You have to they said
We will make you the rings
This one with the snake is for Jupiter
I don't know anything about him I said
But I do like the ring
I don't know anything about him I said

Don't worry they said
He knows all about you

Something soft is brushing my milk drape
Why does my body have to change for the light
I don't know how to do it
Thurgood Marshall
Thornton Wilder
Uma Thurman
Sir Thomas More
I don't know how to do it
Worship the god of persons
Worship the god who lives in the back
Feed him my food
Surrender all my names to him
Know the difference between myself and another
I browse the curds and the grasses
I eat them with my muzzle
I am a cow like Rumi
I am a holy man
I have no idea how to do it
Holy holy holy
Nevertheless I have no choice but to do it
Holy holy holy man

Once you are in the car
You are on the road
Once you are on the road
You are the fool on the spool of God
Your existence is aflame in a scroll of sun
And here you are born
And here you are born again
And here you will ascend into the black mouth of God

I don't know how to do it but I am fuck well doing it
I am doing it
That's life I guess

Of course it can be secular to be alive on a Thursday
And as a matter of fact
It cannot
And as a matter of fact this is between you and me universally
And nothing I say belongs remotely to me

Only one grass whistles out the tooth of my horse
And the moon drops fast behind the fences
And the wheat lolls back
And waits for death

I could see the sea from where I was
My mesh hat shone blue

The jagged cheek of Gibraltar
Solid, sucked in the mouth and never melting
Where my dog's warm underleg soothes the whetstone
I speak of it thusly
I say it thusly
I lisp its name into the curl of wall stained dark in the impression
     of my mouth

Only one grass whistles out the tooth of my horse
And the moon bends back
And the wheat lolls back
And opens its stomach
And waits for death

I soak it in my black water
It seethes in bags I have hung up among the rafters
It seethes in bags of amber and jasper transfusions
Flower liquids in cellophane pouches
Streaked with goo clots of plastic soldier sun

When the pitcher is poured out the length of my tongue
And ten vats of grease ignite in unison

Only one grass whistles out the tooth of my horse
A too-tight phylactory
The moon bending back
The wheat lolling back
Scrollboxes clattering on the stone
Jugs of gasoline and jugs of sand

I threw my coat on the sea
The velvet sea
My coat spread
My coat spread
It was the blue of the top of the column of milk
Its soaked embroidery
It was the ditty two winds whined into the anus of night

Skating along the floor of the brook
Are leaves and ice. Devolving on the brook floor
It is only one little one. One blue shard of pale Palestine.
The wineskins are pricked
Goats' udders banged sore
Where mica lodges in the mucus house

Where my velvet is sucked down
Where the cheek blows thick with sleep to be brushed by the sea
Blue Palestine
Wrung swan neck in oil
Tasseling dirty day with rocks that fly and fly and fall and fall and
    fall.

The moon bends back
And the wheat lolls back

A cracker whitens on the tongue of the hanged man
My velvet is sucked down the sea
The sea wall is chipped blue
The clock of Palestine
Gulls' salt beaks
Iron drums soldered shut and stuffed with salt cod
An anvil of rammed earth in the form of a baby belly button
Hair raised on the hat of the imperatrix
Embossed forever in her brass annal

No grass screams against the foot of my horse
No rock whinnies down the side of the sea
No scroll staves off the reeds quivering in my rib wall
And no algaes quiver
And no frogs belch out the tablet over the song of my purchase
of night
Blue Palestine
Red sucker bloody on the bib of the world
Blue Palestine
Ice tray soaked in solid sun

mystics of youtube

Sophie Robinson

when you turn
32 the planets of the lovers
are in the exact same place
in the sky as they were
when you were born
mars return
venus return
when you went away
i only kept quiet when i ate
do i not even now
have something in my mouth
as i write this
a gummy void   a baby void
my consolations
because i was lovehungry—
when you return
like the moon curving the earth
don't call me
by my name
my milky folds
my pinky folds
my moony face   o this trance im in
i leave myself on read
take a white bath
shave my legs to the top

consult the mystics of youtube
from the tub
nothing lasts forever
so stay a little hungry
so let the void stay empty
so let the moon sway gently
as it comes round the corner
my eyes get stuck on aurora —
everything returns   so i don't have to
moon now reflected
in a wide & round   reservoir of milk
down at the edge of town
further from the sun now   my winter of bad thots
my life in black tshirts   i left me on read again
so i stay a little empty   took off my tshirt again
so i stay a little hungry   a little further from the sun again
so im watching that same film again
so im eating my same feelings again:
pop tart   peanut buttercup
marshmallow shishkabob
                    cheeseball pickmeup

                    ♫ *nothing lasts forever*
                        white ladies! sing to me:
          lorelai gilmore
                    rory gilmore
                              cher

                                        christina ricci

                    winona ryder

                                        madonna

102

madonna

madonna

hi mama

return

Lost to the Phosphorus
Erica Scourti

Έχουμε διαρροή με γυμνό μάτι
διαφορετικές τρύπες
προσπαθώντας να υπάρξουν μέσα σε κλισέ
μια ρομαντική επένδυση στο υπεριώδες φως

Έχω ξεπεράσει τα σύνορά της,
αναγνωρίζοντας ταυτόχρονα
την καρδιά του,
στα έντερα μου

You should never speak in a language
other people don't somaticise in
apart from a few- cute- words
like therapeutic, or yia-yia

But without breathing, νυχτέρια,
it's very rude

How to write an autobiography without breathing?
mia aftoviographia choris logia, ta logia mou,
without my words, or
san tous fílous, erastes and lost devices,
when everything's clean of transitional contagion?

Everybody carries a history,
of πολύτιμα assets contaminated

A crystal campaign of plain English
teaches how to clean off the transferred forces
deposited on the limbs, tongue and spine,
leaving clues behind:
an accent as a technology of access
η προφορά, ως technologia πρόσβασης

I've always felt alienated from my own voice
like only to miso milaei-
but katathlipsei took it clean away

How to write an apotropaic visual device?
That's Greek for 'prophylactic'
προφυλακτικός, like condom
'protective', literally: it 'turns away'
σαν θεραπεία αποστροφής
or 'apotreptic', like that the threat of
negative emotional contagion is 70 bpm

But don't describe what a sham mouth cannot,
We are the lucky ones!
Who speak in a liquid crystal clarity,
who pass, freely, fully Anglo
into the tourismos and hospitality industries

You must have some kind of special feature
incorporated into your identity to be given the evil eye
So it's a kind of komplimento,
a tool of social classification
ένα εργαλείο κοινωνικής ταξινόμησης

Relatives, friends kai oikogenia
are usually responsible for casting it
and the evil eye grows with the transmission
of negative emotions such as zilia

Βασκανία, μάτιασμα ή κακό μάτι
είναι δυνατό να επηρεαστεί αρνητικά
ένας άνθρωπος εξαιτίας μονάχα ενός βλέμματος

Το mati προστατεύει άτομα που είναι
vulnerable, sociable, and distinctive;
operating in the land of προσδοκίες kai
parasites, gossip, and envy-

φτου φτου φτου
να μη σε ματιάξω!
which translates
'I spit so that I won't give you the evil eye'

People with blue eyes- οι γαλανομάτηδες-
are most often accused of casting the mati
especially if they're close to you

Οι πατέρες της εκκλησίας δεν αρνούνται τη βασκανία,
τη θεωρούν όμως, έργο του διαβόλου,
the devil's labour
Pregnant women are considered to be more open and hence,
more vulnerable to the evil eye-
their transitional status makes them more susceptible.

Spatially, thresholds and passageways
tou somatos και του σπιτιού
are sites of potential danger

Thelei kaneis ena wet wipe?

I'm collecting your debris,
your dribbles and drivel
And will hold them up to the granularity of moments
to trade on the viability of your future essence
and monetise the 3d printing of your pneuma

Επιτρέψτε μου λοιπόν να σας φωτίσω:
correct illumination is inevitable,
but that's very intelling
non-toxic, non-hazardous people don't somaticize
you won't ensomatisei
the first time we share everything

I dipped my head down,
under the blacklight, to see forms emerge
we discharge something long held?
it glows bright yellow under UV black light

I dipped my head down,
under the way I'm going to lick you
through the skin as microbes would say
like UV DNA tagging Smartwater
ένα έξυπνο νερό δηλαδή

With each batch of smartwater
bots like germs are scaling up,
channeling viral moods through you
so it becomes impossible to measure
what you've absorbed,
and what its doing to your insides
which translates
'I spit so the criminal is literally carrying
a unique 'data-set' of epidermal evidence'

til the officials show up
with a dummy instead,
faking microbial contamination
with the intention of invisibly monitoring cleaning routines,
cleansing rituals for inner intensities-
surfaces powdered blue
with typical bacteria cells
των καμένων κυττάρων
breathing in the toxicity of their dust

Dust in the blacklit sky
Smart dust in the factories, monitoring machines.
Smart Dust in your body, monitoring your well being.
Smart dust in the absence of genuine friends
whose psycho-enteric responsiveness
quantifies your levels of considering me

I know you've been swallowed by the sand,
με έσυρε το αλάti,
έχετε καταπιεί από την άμμο

What are your symptoms?
he would ask
sweat and salt, ιδρώτα και αλάτι,
and activating and your eyeballs, *all the time*
so organ speech becomes real tears

I want my body so bitter I could show up bare,
throw up in the office of genuine free forms,
so bitter I could puke;
But I just smiled instead,
ένα απλό χαμόγελο
because that's what we do here,
kai αυτοί είναι οι κανόνες

I dropped my soul from death,
my eyes from tears, my feet from falling
translating sound into limbic reactions,
feelings into fat, synaisthimata se lipos;

I say, said all the night sky,
ζωντανό τον νυχτερινό ουρανό
as I idly imagine who speaks both,
without words,
without work,
getting lodged in the manifolds of skin

I just need a speck, μια κουκίδα
and tingling inside me, sparks in the mouth:
Can you quantify a vibe, the water and so on?
like, did you know,
pupil dilation was once used to detect sexual deviance

where openings are pink,
the surfaces behind
believe in the absences uploaded to them-
I can feel another rush coming on!

because When You Or They Think You're Going To Die
They're cursing you
with a "medical hex" called nocebo-
They're not *trying* to harm you
but They harm you anyway
σας βλάπτουν ούτως ή άλλως.

Placebos, diladi to eikoniko farmako
describe sham mourners
hired to sing vespers for the dead
pseftes yia tis teleftaies teletes
the word originally meant parasites, fakes, apateones
koroido

But sugar pills work wonders
as a function of belief
pou metafrazetai:
'your intestines know what you've lost,
even if you don't know you've been sugar-pilled'

Unmanaged expectations, like a microdot
I once tried to take
that got blown away into the sand
but worked anyway
ta ichni sto chrono
ginontai pragmatikotita

Κανείς δεν μιλούσε,
ημασταν χαμένες, γελοίες, lost to it,
chasing microscopic sparks
of bioluminescence into the ink,
as she cleared the water and splashed, and screamed,
I'd believe anything, if it felt right inside!

Το πρωί οι παλιοί γελούσαν,
they said, όλοι οι newbies το κάνουν αυτό
την πρώτη φορά,
first time they see the phosphorus
μας είπανε, *we share everything on this beach,*
including your weed;
που τους βόλευε βέβαια

But there are highs and pains
vrisies bleached green in the surf,
lingering on a vibration that drained out
our hysterics, our histories, our istories
in an all-night fever

Ο fakos φθορίζει την καρδιαρροή
which can be translated as:
'I spit, nights flowing without breathing,
into the abyss with no end'

Not everything interior to the body exteriorises its look,
According to feel how I want his fingers
pushed soft inside me instead-
I'm cursing your hands-
You can't protect

Whatever is yours?
Ό, τι είναι δικό σου;
οτιδήποτε είναι δικό σου, δεν είναι και δικό μου
whatever is yours, is not mine too
ένας εκστατικός αισθητήρας, night fevery interials,
νυχτερινής πτώσης, one soma to another

I can feel another trust rushing on,
I can feel another rush trusting on!
μια άλλη βιασύνη εμπιστοσύνης
comes crashing you down
and only shows up
στο fos που σβήνει

I'm speaking through solar electricity functions,
walking through revenue streams of identity formation,
clicking and licking
and liking and linking,
showing up all the parts
where I felt hollow inside
sweat anything clear,
idrotas katharos
translates:
'I spit, so that meshes written anything left unchecked,
is transferred from death, to you anyway'

πού τα βρήκαμε σκορπισμένα το πρωί
washed up on the beach,
where legend had it that a young man's body
was found in the shallows

Moons orbit around atmospheric changes,
heart racing, this is 100 bpm,
I see faces of friends spin through plastic bottle tops
count layers of substrate in my tattered beach bag
system failures turn sensual systems
into multilayered logics of edible substances

I fumbled for words,
spitting out glots
as I cannibalise my interiors
for external valuation

I wanted to ingest, digest, secrete
process everything down, into smooth paste
instead of starting anew
so why does it all *still* taste of endings?

We learn how to find anything,
on a widened ledge,
or a precarious edge,
a drop down
as I lay watching the Pleiades

'Prosexe' they said, 'mia kopela is lying in the sand'
tracing a clenched fist constellation
that passes hand to heri to mouth,
se stoma, heri se hand se stoma
leaks out of naked eyes

I'm no good at endings- too prone to clichés-
because kaimos, then metaphrasetai-

but I wanted you to come away with something
to hold
a protective shell,
glowing in a sweaty palm
a skinful reminder

Gently illuminated
an exit appears-
she gets up to walk

Even when there are no escape routes,
there's always a fine line to trace,
to burrow through,
remembering tin anapnoi

The Past's Future

Dolly Turing

Open | Sun | Shimmer | Movement
slips between channels,
our experience, energy
moves from
place
to
focus. You, the heavy weight,
tall hoof of the past's
future, you burning neck,
soul inside my heart,
trapped and
breaking
Out, weak point
must be strong to hold
space for you.
The largest
form
an everything
for endless expanse,
still tracking under !Xu's wide sky,
while these layers of
Power struggles
demand sugar in the cement.
For shudders, kicks,
expulsions, pushing towards

our future, our past
presents itself now in threatening letters,
to loved elders,
whose home is here.
Who once welcomed
to Britain
as young folks,
descended from the people
ancestors of this country
stole, sold across oceans as slaves
into the hardest life on
those soft wave shores, the ones who survived
and broke finally free
into a world which has
never yet stopped trampling on those
Bones, those humans, adding
accretion to inheritance
trauma, constant battle ground
to be known
as human, to live in peace,
share in, and hold
wide network of Love and
All, for those ghosts
that haunt the bones, raised each time
Words are spoken or
threats or guns are raised. The Windrush
a n o p e n i n g
of its time, another expectation
of servitude, to previous
powers, now in need. One dressed in

fancy best and invited
for tea, which we drank in your living room
when we were very tiny, so sweet, so
Delicious. My first attempt at a school friend,
I digress. And you know
on a day like this
in 2015 I
wrote about hearing Miriam Makeba
in the sunshine in Brighton,
Our own adventures in community
and amplified political
horror had
just begun. Whirlwind creation
of spitting fire between our hands
You kick and sputter, you
Hoof hands, you heart
neck attack, the world,
the life and
death
oh my. Half a million souls
across the waves to reach these
shores towards attacks, you know the
signs in windows, fists in
faces, words, attitudes,
Integral structures
against
and hopscotch
Imagination games, playing out
Beautiful mergers, our
learning, playing

music, dancing
our attempts to make some sense
of belonging
Together
Apart
to build what we saw,
make magic in the mountains of
our dreams, like, no idea
what the power of stories,
words | breathe | touch
could be. Still. A woven dream of
a moment in the
brutal
Interruption, a vision of a home to make
somewhere. That
somewhere.
It continues, perhaps on purpose
the layers have kept
Pouring in the same patterns in the
mould.
Mold may grow in
Different shapes. We weaponize mold
to grow new forms. If fungus can eat
plastic
we Mycelium are the fungus
that can eat these structures, it is not a drill but a
Growing, and the patterns can be moved through,
Can be adapted or SMASHED
We say NO to this
repeat pattern built of slavery. We say it

with real process inside and outside
of ourselves. We say it with care and love and
Setting fire. We say it throwing seeds and spores in all
Directions and ready to water | wait | tend | protect.
We say it with sigils. We say it with alchemy.
We stand together in our home.
We build that astra
Diane spoke of.
We say it with those we love.
We say it looking
at who we are.
We say it clearly. We say it with words.
We say NO to this
repeat pattern built of colonisation
and slavery.

A Short History of Mythology

Jane Yeh

To be a lady centaur

                               leaping across the Hedgehog Isles

Is to be in heaven

                                 and wearing a tropical lei

Like a shower of spiral curls

                                 my tail is springy

It smells like violets and shit

                                 in a good way

Thank you pool

                                 I can bounce down a peninsula

Laden with Gorgonzola

                                 harvesting bites between watching my shows

And inventing the handsaw

                                 between weaving a tapestry

And visiting space

                                 I will stomp on a few thousand years

Of lady centaur history

                                 without regrets

To leap through a waterfall

                                 in a novelty T-shirt

Holding a gift basket between my teeth

                                 to shake my legs around

Pretending to be a freaky spider

                                 to investigate a mole all day

Or whatever is stealing my tomatoes

                              is a paradise

Like a partridge
                         my head bobs when I run

My boobs bob when I run
                                   when I run into the purple-tinged hills

I can be mythical
                         like the very specific flower

They use in salads in LA
                              as a garnish

If you look at it upside down
                                   you can see the face of a furious boy

Contributors

Kaveh Akbar is the founding editor of *Divedapper*. His poems have appeared in *The New Yorker, Poetry, Tin House, Ploughshares* and elsewhere. The recipient of a 2016 Ruth Lilly and Dorothy Sargent Rosenberg Fellowship from the Poetry Foundation and the Lucille Medwick Memorial Award from the Poetry Society of America, Akbar was born in Tehran, Iran, and currently lives and teaches in Florida.

Rachael Allen was born in Cornwall and studied English Literature at Goldsmiths College. She is the poetry editor at *Granta*, co-editor at the poetry press Clinic and of online journal *Tender*. A pamphlet of her poems was published as part of the Faber New Poets scheme, and her first collection will be published by Faber in 2019. She is the recipient of an Eric Gregory award and New Writing North's Andrew Waterhouse award.

Nuar Alsadir is a poet, essayist and psychoanalyst. She is the author of the poetry collections *Fourth Person Singular* (2017), a finalist for the 2017 National Book Critics Circle Award for Poetry and shortlisted for the 2017 Forward Prize for Best Collection; and *More Shadow Than Bird* (Salt Publishing, 2012). She is a fellow at The New York Institute for the Humanities and works as a psychotherapist and psychoanalyst in private practice in New York.

Khairani Barokka (b. Jakarta, 1985) is a writer, poet and artist in London. She is author and illustrator of poetry-art book *Indigenous*

Species, nominated for a Goldsmiths Public Engagement Award (Tilted Axis Press, 2016), co-editor with Ng Yi-Sheng of *HEAT: A Southeast Asian Urban Anthology* (Fixi, 2016), and co-editor, with Sandra Alland and Daniel Sluman, of *Stairs and Whispers: D/deaf and Disabled Poets Write Back* (Nine Arches Press, 2017), shortlisted for a Saboteur Award for Best Anthology. Her first full-length poetry collection, *Rope*, was published by Nine Arches Press in October 2017.

Emily Berry has published two books of poems, *Dear Boy* (Faber & Faber, 2013) and *Stranger, Baby* (Faber & Faber, 2017). She edits *The Poetry Review* and is a fellow of the Royal Society of Literature.

A. K. Blakemore was born in London in 1991. Twice named a Foyle Young Poet of the Year, her work has been widely published and anthologised, appearing in journals including *Poetry London*, *Poetry Review* and *Ambit*. Her debut collection, *Humbert Summer*, appeared in 2015 and was awarded the Melita Hume Prize. *Fondue* was published by Offord Road Books in July 2018.

Vahni Capildeo's multilingual, cross-genre writing is grounded in time experienced through place. Her DPhil in Old Norse literature and translation theory, her travels, and her Indian diaspora/Caribbean background deepen the voices in the landscapes that inspire her. Her poetry (six books and four pamphlets) includes *Measures of Expatriation*, awarded the Forward Prize for Best Collection in 2016. She has worked in academia; in culture for development, with Commonwealth Writers; and as an Oxford English Dictionary lexicographer. Capildeo held the Judith E. Wilson Poetry Fellowship and the Harper-Wood Studentship at Cambridge. She is currently a Douglas Caster Cultural Fellow at the University of Leeds.

Jen Calleja is a writer and literary translator from German. Her debut poetry collection *Serious Justice* (2016) was published by Test Centre. She has translated literary fiction and non-fiction by many contemporary authors and figures including Wim Wenders, Kerstin Hensel and Gregor Hens. She lives in London.

Kayo Chingonyi was born in Zambia in 1987, and moved to the UK at the age of six. He is the author of two pamphlets, and a fellow of the Complete Works programme for diversity and quality in British Poetry. In 2012, he was awarded a Geoffrey Dearmer Prize, and was Associate Poet at the Institute of Contemporary Arts (ICA) in 2015. His first full-length collection, *Kumukanda* (Chatto & Windus), won a Somerset Maugham Award and the Dylan Thomas Prize 2018. It was shortlisted for the Costa Poetry Prize, Seamus Heaney Centre First Poetry Collection Prize, the Ted Hughes Award for New Work in Poetry, the Roehampton Poetry Prize, and the Jhalak Prize. Kayo is poetry editor for *The White Review* and an Assistant Professor of Creative Writing at Durham University.

Dr. Elinor Cleghorn is a writer working across feminist visual cultures, histories of medicine, and narrative poetry. Her critical scholarship has been published in journals including *'Screen', The Moving Image Review* and *Art Journal*. She was shortlisted for the Fitzcarraldo Editions essay prize 2017, and is currently writing a research memoir about autoimmunity. Her debut poetry pamphlet, *lupercalia*, was published by Litmus Press last year. Elinor can be found at www.theunwellwoman. com

CAConrad is the author of nine books of poetry and essays. *While Standing in Line for Death* (Wave Books), received the 2018 Lambda

Award. A recipient of a Pew Fellowship in the Arts, they also received The Believer Magazine Book Award and The Gil Ott Book Award. They teach regularly at Sandberg Art Institute in Amsterdam, and their books, essays, films, interviews, rituals and other publications can be found online at http://CAConrad.blogspot.com

Nia Davies was born in Sheffield and studied English at the University of Sussex. She has been editor of *Poetry Wales* since 2014. Her pamphlets, *Then Spree* (Salt, 2012), *Çekoslovakyalıla tıramadıklarımızdanmısınız or Long Words* (Boiled String, 2016) and *England* (Crater, 2017), were followed by her first book-length collection, *All fours* (Bloodaxe Books, 2017), shortlisted for the Roland Mathias Poetry Award 2018 (Wales Book of the Year Awards). *Interversions* (Poetrywala, 2018) documents a collaboration with Kannada poet Mamta Sagar and *Key Blank* is out from the Literary Pocket Book series in 2018. She is currently undertaking practice-based research into poetry and ritual at the University of Salford.

Kate Duckney studied at UEA for both her BA (English Literature with Creative Writing) and her MA (Poetry). She has been published in *Ambit, Clinic, Zarf, The Literateur* and *Ink, Sweat and Tears*. Her first collection of poetry, *ada in the shells*, is available with Knives Forks and Spoons Press and her upcoming pamphlet of 'twitter poetry', *@babtriggy*, is forthcoming with if a leaf falls press. She lives and works in London.

Livia Franchini is a writer and translator from Tuscany, Italy. Selected publications include *The White Review, Hotel* and the anthologies *On Bodies* (3 of Cups) and *Wretched Strangers* (Boiler House Press). She has translated Natalia Ginzburg, Sam Riviere, James Tiptree Jr. and

Michael Donaghy among many others. Livia is one of the inaugural writers-in-residence of the Connecting Emerging Literary Artist project. She is currently at work on her first novel, as part of a funded PhD at Goldsmiths.

Will Harris is an Assistant Editor at *The Rialto* and a fellow of The Complete Works III. He is the author of the poetry chapbook, *All this is implied,* and the essay, *Mixed-Race Superman.*

Caspar Heinemann is a writer, artist, and poet. Their interests include critical occultism, gay biosemiotics, and countercultural mythologies. They have exhibited at the Museum of Modern Art in Warsaw, David Roberts Art Foundation, London, and Outpost Gallery, Norwich. They were born in London, UK, roughly 2.5 months after the release of Green Day's seminal album *Dookie.*

Lucy Ives is the author of the novel *Impossible Views of the World.* Her writing has appeared in *Art in America, Artforum, the Baffler, Granta, Lapham's Quarterly, Vogue,* and newyorker.com. For five years she was an editor with the online magazine *Triple Canopy.* A graduate of Harvard and the Iowa Writers' Workshop, she holds a Ph.D. in comparative literature from New York University. She currently teaches in the Image Text interdisciplinary MFA program at Ithaca College and is editing a collection of writings by the artist Madeline Gins.

Rebecca May Johnson is a writer and literary curator living in London. Her writing has appeared in the *TLS, LRB blog, The Financial Times, Guardian, Vogue* and many other publications. She is co-founder and curator of 'Voices at The Table' and co-curates 'Sitting Room', a long-running series of readings. She created the Food Memory Bank, a digital project to collect public memory about food and eating. Rebecca recently completed a PhD about a contemporary feminist reworking of *The Odyssey* at UCL and works as researcher into literature and translation at Newcastle University. She is writing a book of public philosophy that takes food as its tool to think with.

Bhanu Kapil is a British-Indian artist and poet. She is the author of five full-length works of poetry/prose: *The Vertical Interrogation of Strangers* (2001), *Incubation: a space for monsters* (2006), *humanimal [a project for future children]* (2009), *Schizophrene* (2011), and *Ban en Banlieue* (2015). She lives in Colorado where she teaches Interdisciplinary Studies at Naropa University.

Amy Key's first collection *Luxe* was published by Salt in 2013. She is the author of two pamphlets *Instead of Stars* (Tall Lighthouse) and *History* (If A Leaf Falls Press). Her poems have been widely published in magazines and anthologies including *Poetry, The Poetry Review, Best British Poetry 2015* (Salt), *Poetry Please* (Faber & Faber) and *The Poetry of Sex* (Penguin). Her second book-length collection, *Isn't Forever*, a Poetry Book Society Wild Card Choice, was published by Bloodaxe in June 2018. From Spring 2018–Spring 2019 she is joint poet-in-residence, alongside Rebecca Perry, at Halsway Manor, the National Centre for Folk Arts.

Daisy Lafarge is a writer, artist and editor based in Edinburgh. *understudies for air* was published by Sad Press Poetry in 2017. Daisy received an Eric Gregory Award in 2017, and was shortlisted for the 2018 Edwin Morgan Poetry Award. She is reviews editor at MAP, a commissioning and publishing project for artist-led production based in Glasgow.

Dorothea Lasky is the author of five full-length collections of poetry: *Milk* (Wave Books, 2018), *Rome* (Liveright/W.W. Norton, 2014), *Thunderbird* (Wave Books, 2012), *Black Life* (Wave Books, 2010), and *AWE* (Wave Books, 2007). She is also the author of six chapbooks, including *Matter: A Picturebook* (Argos Books, 2012), *The Blue Teratorn* (Yes Yes Books, 2012) and *Poetry is Not a Project* (Ugly Duckling Presse, 2010). Born in St. Louis in 1978, her poems have appeared in *American Poetry Review, Boston Review, Paris Review,* among other places. She is the co-editor of *Open the Door: How to Excite Young People About Poetry* (McSweeney's, 2013) and is a 2013 Bagley Wright Lecturer on Poetry. Currently, she is an Assistant Professor of Poetry at Columbia University's School of the Arts and lives in New York City.

Ursula K. Le Guin was one of the finest writers of our time. Her books have attracted millions of devoted readers and won many awards, including the National Book Award, the Hugo and Nebula Awards and a Newbery Honor. Among her novels, *The Left Hand of Darkness, The Dispossessed* and the six books of Earthsea have attained undisputed classic status; and her recent series, the Annals of the Western Shore, has won her the PEN Center USA Children's literature award and the Nebula Award for best novel. In 2014 Ursula Le Guin was awarded the National Book Foundation Medal for Distinguished Contribution to American Letters. She lived in Portland, Oregon, until she passed away in January 2018.

Francesca Lissette was born on the outskirts of London in 1987. Xir first book *Teens* was published by Mountain Press (2012); Lisette's second book, *sub-rosa, or, The Book of Metaphysics* is forthcoming from Boiler House Press in 2018. Xir solo performance piece *TO MAKE MANIFEST: AN UNDOING* was presented at KN Raum für Kunst

(Berlin) in 2017. Lisette offers creative spiritual counselling through astrology, tarot, somatics and ritual, as the Glitter Oracle.

Writer, editor, educator, activist and critic, **Canisia Lubrin** has had work published and anthologized widely, including in *Brick, Vallum, The Puritan, Arc, Toronto Star, Best Canadian Poetry in English 2018* and *The Unpublished City,* nominated for the 2018 Toronto Book Award. Her fiction has been nominated for the Puschart prize. She holds an MFA in creative writing from the University of Guelph. Her multiple award-nominated debut collection is *Voodoo Hypothesis* (Wolsak and Wynn, 2017). She lives in Whitby, Ontario.

So Mayer is a writer and activist. Recent works include *Political Animals: The New Feminist Cinema* (IB Tauris), *(O)* (Arc) and *<jacked a kaddish>* (Litmus). They work with queer feminist film curation collective Club des Femmes. @troublemayer

Karen McCarthy Woolf was born in London to an English mother and a Jamaican father. She is the recipient of a Glenna Luschei/Prairie Schooner editors' award and holds a doctorate from Royal Holloway, University of London for her research into diversifying ecocritical discourse and new ways of writing about nature, the city and the sacred. Her celebrated début *An Aviary of Small Birds* was shortlisted for the 2015 Felix Dennis Prize for Best First Collection and the Fenton Aldeburgh First Collection Prize, as well as being a *Guardian* Book of the Year and a Poetry Book Society Recommendation. Her latest collection *Seasonal Disturbances* (2017) is a PBS Recommendation. Karen is the editor of several literary anthologies, most recently *Ten: Poets of the New Generation* (Bloodaxe, 2017).

Lucy Mercer's poems have been published in *Poetry Review, Poetry London* and *The White Review* amongst others. In 2017 she was the winner of the inaugural White Review Poet's Prize. She is studying for a PhD in 'Speculative Emblematics'.

Born in the Mekong Delta and raised in the Washington, D.C. area, **Hoa Nguyen** is the author of five books of poetry, including *As Long As Trees Last* and *Red Juice*. Her book *Violet Energy Ingots*, also from Wave Books, received a 2017 Griffin Prize for poetry nomination. She teaches poetics in several university settings and in a popular long-running, private workshop.

Rebecca Perry's first book-length collection, *Beauty/Beauty* (Bloodaxe Books, 2015), was a Poetry Book Society Recommendation, won the Michael Murphy Memorial Prize 2017, and was also shortlisted for the T.S. Eliot Prize, the Fenton Aldeburgh First Collection Prize and the Seamus Heaney Centre for Poetry Prize for First Full Collection. Rebecca also has a pamphlet, *cleanliness of rooms and walls*, with If A Leaf Falls Press. She was as a Writer Fellow at Manchester University in 2016. She lives and works in London.

Nat Raha is a poet and trans / queer activist, living in Edinburgh, Scotland. She is the author of numerous pamphlets and three collections of poetry: *of sirens / body & faultlines* (Boiler House Press, forthcoming), *countersonnets* (Contraband Books, 2013), and *Octet* (Veer Books, 2010). She is currently completing a PhD in queer Marxism and contemporary poetry at the University of Sussex. In 2017, Nat's essay 'Transfeminine Brokenness, Radical Transfeminism' appeared in the South Atlantic Quarterly, and she is the co-editor of *Radical Transfeminism* zine.

Nisha Ramayya is a poet and lecturer in Creative Writing at Queen Mary, University of London. Her pamphlets *Notes on Sanskrit* (2015) and *Correspondences* (2016) are published by Oystercatcher Press. *Threads*, a creative-critical pamphlet co-authored with Sandeep Parmar and Bhanu Kapil, is published by clinic. She is a member of the 'Race & Poetry & Poetics in the UK' research group and the interdisciplinary practice-as-research group Generative Constraints.

Ariana Reines is the author of *The Cow* (Alberta Prize 2006), *Coeur de Lion* (2007), *Mercury* (2011), & *A Sand Book* (forthcoming 2019 from Tin House). Her Obie-winning play *TELEPHONE* was commissioned by The Foundry Theatre in 2009 & published in 2018 by Wonder. She has created performances for The Whitney Museum of American Art, Swiss Institute, Stuart Shave/Modern Art, the Solomon R. Guggenheim Museum, & many others, & performs & teaches around the world. A Visiting Critic at Yale, she astrologizes at lazyeyehaver.com.

Sophie Robinson is a poet. She lives between London and Norwich, where she teaches Creative Writing at the University of East Anglia. Her new book *Rabbit* is forthcoming from Boiler House Press in November 2018.

Erica Scourti is an artist and writer based in London and Athens. Her work mines personal archives to explore performative, collaborative autobiography across multiple somatotechnic registers. She is currently undertaking a PhD at Goldsmiths, London.

Sarah Shin is a publisher and curator. She is the creator of New Suns: A Feminist Literary Festival, and is a co-founder and director of the Silver Press and Ignota Books. She works at Verso Books.

Rebecca Tamás is a poet currently based in York, where she works as a Lecturer at York St John University. Her most recent pamphlet, *Savage*, came out from Clinic Press in 2017, and was an LRB Bookshop pamphlet of the year, and a Poetry School Book of the Year. Her first collection, *WITCH*, focusing on feminist language and occult practice, will be out from Penned in the Margins in 2019.

Dolly Turing is sometimes Dolly Dollycore and experiments with poetry, sound and movement to create rituals. Their current growing, evolving work *Quest(ion)* is a poetic ritual about places, movement, connections, attachment, interruption, otherworlds, wide open space, spirits, stories and nothingness. She has had work published by *Datableed*, *The Winter Olympiks* and *Litmus*.

Jane Yeh was born in America and has lived in London since 2002. She holds degrees from Harvard, Iowa, Manchester Metropolitan, and Royal Holloway London universities. Her first collection of poems, *Marabou* (Carcanet, 2005), was shortlisted for the Whitbread, Forward, and Aldeburgh poetry prizes. She was named a Next Generation poet by the Poetry Book Society for her second collection, *The Ninjas* (Carcanet, 2012). Her third collection, *Discipline*, is forthcoming from Carcanet in 2019.